MANAGING

G000113641

Managing Universities and Colleges: Guides to Good Practice

Series editors:

David Warner, Principal and Chief Executive, Swansea Institute of Higher Education

David Palfreyman, Bursar and Fellow, New College, Oxford

This series has been commissioned in order to provide reference manuals of good practice on the major areas of the management of colleges and universities.

MANAGING STUDENTS

John M. Gledhill

Open University Press
Buckingham · Philadelphia

Open University Press
Celtic Court
22 Ballmoor
Buckingham
MK18 1XW

email: enquiries@openup.co.uk
world wide web: http://www.openup.co.uk

and
325 Chestnut Street
Philadelphia, PA 19106, USA

First Published 1999

ISBN   0 335 20257 8 (hb)   0 335 20256 X (pb)

A catalogue record of this book is available from the British Library

Library of Congress Cataloging-in-Publication Data
Gledhill, John M., 1948–
    Managing students / John M. Gledhill.
        p.   cm. – (Managing colleges and universities)
    Includes bibliographical references and index.
    ISBN 0-335-20257-8 (hardbound). – ISBN 0-335-20256-X (pbk.)
    1. Education. Higher–Great Britain–Administration.   2. Deans
(Education)–Great Britain.   3. Student affairs services–Great Britain–
Administration.   I. Title.   II. Series.
LB2341.8.G7G54   1999
378. 1'01–dc21
                                                                98-29066
                                                                CIP

Typeset by Graphicraft Limited, Hong Kong
Printed in Great Britain by St Edmundsbury Press Limited,
Bury St Edmunds, Suffolk

This book is dedicated to Niccolò Machiavelli,
the first great pragmatic manager (see also Jay 1987).

CONTENTS

How managers are involved with recruitment,
and how to avoid fraud; how to balance the needs
of students and management at enrolment and
induction; how to look after their needs during
and after their studies.

Whether it matters how a course is constructed,
and how courses should be managed for the benefit
of students.

How to know what students are doing, keep it
painless for them from beginning to end, and how
to constrain cheating.

FOREWORD

Educational administration is not solely about students, but an efficient student administration is one of the central aims of all institutions. The past 20 years have seen a fair number of erudite analyses of educational trends, and the management of national and local educational policy. What has been conspicuously lacking is a 'hands-on' manual for users: a handbook of management and administrative techniques which can be used and referred to by all those involved in student administration. Student administration is now very different from where it was within the living memory of most senior academic and administrative staff when they were themselves students. The straightforward termly roll call and signing on is no longer adequate for what are today large businesses with an annual turnover of several hundred million pounds, and with responsibilities to very demanding governmental and quasi-statutory statistical agencies.

As in business, so in education – the administration should be as unintrusive as possible. That is not to say that there is little to do; more that those tasks which have to be done but which are not part of the core business of education should be done with as little disruption as possible to those at the 'chalk face'. Not all of the student administration is carried out by administrators or managers: academic staff have, sometimes to their great discomfort, an increasing role to play in the administration of their students. That is not a way of sharing out the administrative work among more people, in the hope that this will make it less onerous, but a recognition of the fact that in today's information-rich environment if any members of the institution want to receive helpful, accurate and complete student information out of the records, they almost inevitably have a responsibility for ensuring that the information gets on to the records in the first place. For academic staff this may mean attendance monitoring and checking enrolment details. For administrative staff, whether central or departmental, it involves considerably more.

I have found within this handbook, aimed as it is at those employed in college and university administration, a rich tapestry of detail and a survival manual. Academic staff will benefit from browsing through it, as will those managers who have reached senior positions via routes not involving detailed work with students. In my role as school dean I have to be both an academic leader and a manager. It is a great comfort to me to know that much of the complex detail of the student administration of the institution in which I work is understood and managed as well as this book shows. Of course, it cannot cover everything which the average student administrator learns in a lifetime of this enjoyable work (and I am reliably informed that most of them do actually enjoy it), but nevertheless if you wish to be a successful student administrator you will not go far wrong if you follow the tips given here. I commend it to all those working in education.

Paul D. Hartley, PhD
Dean, School of International Studies and Law,
Coventry University

SERIES EDITORS' INTRODUCTION

Post-secondary educational institutions can be viewed from a variety of different perspectives. For the majority of students and staff who work in them, they are centres of learning and teaching where the participants are there by choice and consequently, by and large, work very hard. Research has always been important in some higher education institutions, but in recent years this emphasis has grown and what for many was a great pleasure and, indeed a treat, is becoming more of a threat and an insatiable performance indicator which just has to be met. Maintaining the correct balance between quality research and learning/teaching, while the unit of resource continues to decline inexorably, is one of the key issues facing us all. Educational institutions as workplaces must be positive and not negative environments.

From another aspect, post-secondary educational institutions are clearly communities, functioning to all intents and purposes like small towns and internally requiring and providing a similar range of services, while also having very specialist needs. From yet another, they are seen as external suppliers of services to industry, commerce and the professions. These 'customers' receive, *inter alia*, a continuing flow of well qualified fresh graduates with transferable skills, part-time and short course study opportunities through which to develop existing employees, consultancy services to solve problems and help expand business, and research and development support to create new breakthroughs.

However, educational institutions are also significant businesses in their own right. One recent study of the economic impact of higher education in Wales shows that it is of similar importance in employment terms to the steel or banking/finance sectors. Put another way, Welsh higher education institutions (HEIs) spend half a billion pounds annually and create more than 23,000 full-time equivalent jobs. And it must be remembered that there are only 13 HEIs in Wales, compared with 175 in the whole of the UK, and that these Welsh institutions are, on average, relatively small. In addition, it has recently been realized that UK HE is a major export industry with the added benefit of long-term financial and political returns. If the UK further education sector is also added to this equation, then the economic impact of post-secondary education is of truly startling proportions.

Whatever perspective you take, it is obvious that educational institutions require managing and, consequently, this series has been produced to facilitate that end. The editors have striven to identify authors who are distinguished practitioners in their own right and, indeed, can also write. The authors have been given the challenge of producing essentially practical handbooks which combine appropriate theory and contextual material with many examples of good practice and guidance.

The topics chosen are of key importance to educational management and stand at the forefront of current debate. Some of these topics have never been covered in depth before and all of them are equally applicable to further as well as higher education. The editors are firmly of the belief that the UK distinction between these sectors will continue to blur and will be replaced, as in many other countries, by a continuum where the management issues are entirely common.

For well over a decade, both the series editors have been involved with a management development programme for senior staff from HE institutions throughout the world. Every year the participants quickly learn that we share the same problems and that similar solutions are normally applicable. Political and cultural differences may on occasion be important, but are often no more than an overlying veneer. Hence, this series will be of considerable relevance and value to post-secondary educational managers in many countries.

We are pleased that this launch volume in the series covers a vital area in the management of any educational institution: the mechanics of registering, teaching, examining and graduating the students. It is this activity, which is inevitably routine and necessarily repetitive, which is often overlooked and undervalued by those concentrating on more glamorous 'developmental' and 'entrepreneurial' ventures. Yet it is at least embarrassing and potentially disastrous if it goes wrong – if fees are not collected, if the teaching timetable disintegrates, if exam marks are lost, if the wrong degrees are marked, if data protection legislation is neglected, if student appeals are mishandled

... John Gledhill has spent more than 25 years making student administration work in three HEIs – here he instils that experience and expertise into the first full-length treatment of this little-studied but important aspect of institutional management.

David Warner
David Palfreyman

ACKNOWLEDGEMENTS

I would like to give sincere acknowledgement to many years' experience at Hatfield Polytechnic (now the University of Hertfordshire), the University of Warwick and Coventry University, especially to those academic and administrative colleagues who have shown that bureaucracy need not be boring. And to all fellow academic registrars for answering interminable requests for information about how they run their own institutions. Plus, of course, my indefatigable proof-reader.

1

INTRODUCTION

Where there is much desire to learn, there of necessity will be much arguing, much writing, many opinions.

(John Milton, Areopagitica)

Whate'er is best administer'd is best.

(Alexander Pope, An Essay on Man, Ep. iii (1733), I.303)

1.1 The aim of this book

The rise of the student administrator as a profession has gone hand in hand with the expansion of higher education into a mass system. Although there have been many excellent studies on the larger questions of global policy and institutional structure and management, there has been relatively little on the day to day managerial aspects of working with students as an administrator.

This book is not a treatise on the administration of universities (see Lockwood and Davies 1985; Warner and Palfreyman 1996), nor that of higher education in general (see Becher and Kogan 1992; Smith and Webster 1997), nor a history of universities or higher education in the United Kingdom or any other country. Nor does it provide a detailed coverage on student recruitment or admissions policy. What is attempted is a discussion of the principal issues which confront managers and administrators involved with students in their daily work, or in those tasks which come round less frequently but on a periodic and regular basis.

Every institution is different; most solutions are different. Nevertheless, there are many factors which are common to all institutions at all levels. The notes, guidelines and tips included in this book draw on experience of a wide variety of these tasks, and also try to give some necessary background details behind the most common approaches. There are few rights and wrongs; many institutions run perfectly well along different lines from those which may be recommended at various parts of these notes. Conversely, this book cannot serve as a training manual on specific tasks such as the servicing of boards of examiners or the construction of student record systems.

Many of the topics covered here could each be expanded to a lengthy treatise in its own right by experts in those areas. Such extensive detail is not the aim of this book. Similarly, there are extensive legal implications to many of the questions raised here, a large proportion of which have not been satisfactorily decided by the courts (see Farrington 1998; Palfreyman and Warner 1998).

Above all, there is no discussion of pedagogic matters such as teaching, learning, assessment or syllabus construction, except inso-far as it affects administration (see Eastcott and Farmer 1996). It is, of course, risky to detach the academic decision made on a question of principle from the practicalities of implementing it. Too often the administrator is left feeling reminded of Aesop's fable 'Belling the Cat', where the wise owl decided that the best solution for the mice to hear the cat approaching was for one of them to hang a bell round its neck; the solution is good as a theory, but the practical implications for the mice render it impossible to implement and therefore rather ineffective. As in the world outside education, there is no point in the academic decision-makers making a policy decision in a vacuum, as if the owl were to say, 'Look, my job is just to determine the policy, it's up to you to work out how to implement it.'

The main chapters cover areas which are clearly within student administration, such as examinations, awards and pastoral care. Other chapters cover external factors such as legal obligations and data protection, and some student-related aspects of matters such as course construction.

1.2 Who is this book for?

This book is aimed both at the career administrator and at the academic staff member whose duties include any aspect of student administration within higher education. With the exception of the pure researcher, there are few academic staff who can be excused all administration of student matters, even if it only means monitoring attendance in their classes. Nor is it now seen as a waste of valuable academic time for tutors to be involved with administration (though many of them may challenge this view), since an awareness of the implications of many student activities may enhance tutors' under-standing of the way their charges and their institution actually work, to the mutual benefit of all. Students too may find that some parts of this book explain why institutions make what can appear to be unsympathetic decisions, or implement over-complex procedures for simple tasks.

1.3 Global solutions

There are no global solutions. The tips included here are based on many years' experience in a variety of institutions. That does not mean that all wisdom on student administration is covered here, nor that a solution to all problems will be found here. There are few rights and even fewer wrongs. Those who read the various comments will find that a recurring theme is that the actual solution may matter less than the consistency with which it is carried out, and that in many areas (e.g. awards ceremonies) it does not matter at all how an institution chooses to arrange its affairs.

No assumptions have been made about whether the management of the institution is centralized or devolved to academic departments, or has any particular management structure (unitary, binary etc.). The only assumption that has been made is that there will be some sort of central administration and some sort of devolved departmental administration; the allocation of duties and responsibilities between these two is not relevant to these notes or most of the solutions offered.

1.4 Terminology

Terminology is very local. A decision had to be made on how to refer here to structures, bodies, committees, posts, officers etc. Many terms are used for essentially the same activities in different institutions. The intention was to find terms which are reasonably neutral and do not presuppose that the discussion centres on universities rather than colleges (though sometimes this was unavoidable), or on the United Kingdom rather than other countries.

The following conventions should be noted:

- 'Faculty' includes 'school' (and is in any case a better term as it avoids confusion with secondary schools).
- 'Department' refers both to academic departments and to support departments, unless specifically qualified otherwise or the context makes it clear.
- 'Local' means departmental when compared to central, or a partner college when compared to the parent institution.

- 'Dean' refers to the person in charge of a faculty, irrespective of whether it is an elected post, a permanent post or a post held by rotation, and irrespective of the actual title held ('director' would refer to the person in charge of any administrative or support department).
- 'Institution' refers to any type of higher education institution at which people study – university, college, institute etc.
- 'Module' means any self-contained unit of study which forms part of a course; its use here does not presuppose that it is part of a 'modular scheme'.
- 'Assessment' and 'examination' are treated as synonyms unless qualified by some term such as 'written' (in some institutions 'examination' is the global term and 'assessment' means 'coursework'; in others 'assessment' is the global term and 'examination' means 'written examination').
- 'Enrolment' and 'registration' are treated as synonyms, though only the latter is used to refer to registration on individual modules; and
- 'Award' or 'award title' is the qualification or its abbreviation ('BA', etc.); 'course title' is the subject name attached to it ('French', etc.); some cases are hybrid (e.g. undifferentiated 'Bachelor of Laws'), and 'award' may also be used to refer to the combination of award and course title.

2

RECRUITMENT, RETENTION AND AFTERCARE

How managers are involved with recruitment, and how to avoid fraud; how to balance the needs of students and management at enrolment and induction; how to look after their needs during and after their studies.

No admittance till the week after next.
> (Lewis Carroll, *Through the Looking-Glass*, Chapter 9)

In the catalogue ye go.
> (William Shakespeare, *Macbeth*, III.i.92)

Hast thou no care of me?
> (William Shakespeare, *Antony and Cleopatra*, IV.xiii.60)

But, O the heavy change, now thou art gone.
> (John Milton, *Lycidas*, 1.37)

2.1 Who does the recruitment?

Without recruitment policies institutions cannot survive. In the times when applicants vastly outnumbered places available it was possible simply to advertise a course and sign up the best applicants. Few courses can manage this in a mass education system. The best recruitment policies involve all parts of the institution: the public relations section can assess the best strategies, the tutors can advise on the niche for the course and the best specialist advertising media, the administration can facilitate the provision of good records systems for current applicants and good historical data for analysing previous trends. What is unlikely to work well is expecting one person to have strengths in all the above aspects.

It matters little whether recruitment is coordinated centrally or is devolved to individual academic departments: what does matter is the overall efficiency of the operation, and it is up to each institution to devise its own way of doing this within the context of its own structure.

For very similar reasons there is probably less difference than some imagine between the methods adopted for recruiting different types of student: undergraduate/postgraduate, taught/research, agency/direct applicants, local/national/international, full-time/part-time/short course etc. In each of these the basic recruitment tactics apply, i.e. information, communication, knowledge of the market: only the emphases differ.

2.2 Who do you recruit?

All admissions tutors want to fill their courses with the best students; the definition of 'best' may vary according to the aims of the course and the mission of the institution, but it will normally include as a basic criterion that the student has a reasonable expectation of successfully completing the course.

Too often recruitment ideals are masked by pressures of government funding. Giving in to this and recruiting weak students is ill-judged, and in the long run doomed to backfire on the institution. Not only does the institution find it has large drop-out rates (which can be used as adverse publicity), but it is also very poor customer service to the students themselves: coercion of uncertain students on to courses in which they have little interest leads to unwelcome lack of interest and weak performance, and institutional policies and rewards must not be drawn up in a way which encourages this.

Because so much of recruitment policy is driven by government funding methodologies and institutional missions, the method of actually administering the institution's recruitment matters less.

2.3 Who are you interviewing?

Pressure on places, social and family pressures for educational achievement, personal desires to be resident in a particular location, pecuniary advantage: all of these and many other pressures entice some students to commit fraud during their application. It behoves those carrying out the recruitment, and especially those involved in interviewing applicants, to ensure, for example, that the person being interviewed is the same person as the one who turns up at enrolment: impersonation at interview is far from rare, especially with applicants from another country who feel that they may be weak in the local language, or in cases where the interview is very detailed almost to the extent of being an entrance examination.

Any students who are discovered to have deceived the institution as part of their recruitment should be expelled, no matter how good they turn out to be in their own right; to do otherwise sends signals that there is nothing to be lost by trying such fraud. This applies not only to the impersonation cases mentioned above, but also to the presumably much more common cases of misrepresentation of entry qualifications. Academic institutions have a long record of taking on trust everything which applicants put on their forms, and regarding as irrelevant any fraud committed by a student who turns out to be able to cope with the course anyway. If such cases were simply isolated cases of personal desperation this might be understandable, but in many cases the fraud is calculated or even part of a wider organized fraud ring.

2.4   Enrolment: the traditional model

Enrolment used to be just queue, sign, get your grant, go away. Then came computers. The queues became longer, but the system stayed essentially the same. The computers were used as a way of collecting more data (and, with any luck, more information) about the students rather than as a way of speeding up the exercise. This increase in the complexity of enrolment was driven to a very large extent by the increasingly detailed demands of centralized national statistical agencies: the ability to analyse data leads ineluctably to the demand for more data to analyse, irrespective (in many cases) of the actual value of the data.

The natural consequence of this is that the computers are now a virtual necessity for enrolment, but the process itself is little if any quicker than it would have been 20 or 30 years ago. Nor is there any additional time for enrolment itself, despite there being many more students, since it is usually unacceptable to earmark more than one week for enrolment within the teaching timetable.

Possibly encouraged in part by the additional complexity which computerized systems can handle, the ever-widening variety of course structures (see Chapter 3) has also made enrolment more complex.

2.5 Enrolment statistics ▌

Under the traditional manual (or partly computerized) system, the management information was limited, or late. Probably all that could be reasonably expected was a table of enrolment numbers, probably broken down by course and study year. The current demands of management information require virtually instant tabulations of the enrolment statistics, not only in the traditional 'course/year' format which is needed to check that enrolment projections are up to expectations, but also in formats usable for marketing. Analyses, graphs, maps and images show student recruitment (and, presumably, demand) in terms of location of home address, ethnicity, age band, sex, entry qualifications (type, level and 'score') and school/college. The interpretation of these can be problematic: does a blank area on the map of where students are recruited indicate that the institution has not yet tapped that market (and should do so), or does it actually mean that there is no demand in that area and any further marketing would be wasteful? Further analysis may be required to get the correct interpretation.

If any student number contracts are enforced strictly, the need to monitor enrolment against the number of students expected leads to demands for virtually instant statistics by institutional management. Unfortunately it is not possible simply to computerize students themselves, so their enrolments still have to be processed in one form or another – whether this is done centrally, departmentally or as some sort of self-enrolment, the fact that they have enrolled still has to be entered on to the records. The enrolment period is probably the most data-intensive part of the year, even more than the examinations processes.

Although enrolment is a very demanding process for the staff involved, it is also a frustrating time for students. It is, of course, arguable that queuing and confusion are an essential part of peer-bonding: many friendships are struck during enrolment; grumbling about 'the administration' is part of growing up as a student. However, this frustration should be minimized in the interests of 'customer care', and alternative methods of enrolment are well worth exploring fully.

One of the major irritations for students at enrolment is multiple-queuing: queuing to enrol, then queuing to pay fees, then queuing for accommodation etc. This can be reduced by the so-called 'one stop shop' approach: only one queue, no requeuing or diversions, all transactions done at the same time. This implies that all the support services are there too: registry and finance as the main priority, but also, where appropriate, accommodation, students union, grant and loan distribution.

2.6 Alternative approaches to enrolment ■

Central enrolment and departmental enrolment are not radically different. The latter can, in some circumstances, lead to an undesirable separation of enrolment from fee-payment unless there are also local facilities for handling payment; there can also, under pressure, be an inclination not to take as great care with data only required by 'the centre' rather than by the academic department itself, which in turn can increase the amount of post-enrolment chasing.

On-line enrolment can be considered if there is adequate access to computers by students, whether in the institution, at home, or in their workplace; access can be via dial-in lines or through Internet pages with a facility for forms. It can be either self-enrolment where the students work their way unaided through a series of enrolment screens before their access to facilities (library, etc.) is enabled; or it can be run as a group activity with administrators entering the data direct on to the screen in conjunction with the student. The main consideration is whether doing it as a paperless exercise enables the 'contract' with the student (see Chapter 8) to be enforced, if there is no actual signature.

2.7 Part-time student enrolment ■

Students who are attending full-time can be asked to enrol during their normal study week in the safe assumption that this will coincide with the normal working week of the administrative and tutorial staff involved. This is not always the case with part-time students, or the students on the many other variations of course structures (see Chapter 3). The dilemma is to balance the expectation of students who only attend at specific times that they can enrol at or near their normal time (though preferably in a way that does not entail a loss of actual teaching time), even if the staff have to work at unusual hours, against the expectation of the staff that the students should not always expect the whole administration to adjust itself to their separate and varied needs. An alternative which can sometimes work is to have a 'part-time enrolment day' at the weekend, though this can also be unpopular if students have to come in specially just to enrol. Whatever the policy, it should be enforced firmly but with sympathy – either with the staff involved or with the students enrolling.

2.8 Partner colleges' enrolment ■

Students taking courses which are offered at a partner college usually enrol according to the procedures and schedules of the college at which they are attending. This is partly for pragmatic reasons of making it easier for the students and staff, but also for political reasons of not giving the partner college the feeling that it has no control over the administration of these students.

2.9 Enrolment fraud prevention ◼

The possibility of fraud at the recruitment stage has been mentioned. Enrolment, or the post-enrolment processes, should also be used to verify entry qualifications of new students. It may not be practical to check certificates at enrolment itself, but they must be verified at some stage before too much of the term has gone by: it is vital when checking certificates, whether for academic qualifications or for immigration, to make sure that the original copies are seen, not photocopies, as it is very easy to alter many documents. As many as possible of these should be checked with the issuing authority, even if it is one of the well known establishments: fraudsters often deliberately pick bogus qualifications from large institutions on the assumption that it might be harder for them to be sure that they have not lost the records.

2.10 ID cards ◼

ID cards add their own complexity. Reissuing them every year is safest but is time consuming; issuing them for the lifetime of the courses can leave students who withdraw early with cards implying that they are still students. The issuing process may also be made more complicated if smart cards of some sort are used, rather than just photo ID cards. These considerations may mean that the cards have to be issued separately from enrolment.

It is very difficult to enforce any regulation that insists on the ID card being handed in at the end of the student's time at the institution: students who wish to keep their card, whether out of nostalgia or for possible fraudulent use, will simply claim that they have lost it. This can be enforced to some extent by requiring students to lodge a deposit for the card at the start which can be refunded on return of the card. These systems can, however, be burdensome to administer.

2.11 Module registration ◼

In course structures where students have flexibility in their choice of modules or options (see Chapter 3), these may not be fixed in time for the details to be entered at the time of enrolment. This can make it difficult to complete a 'one stop shop' described above, since the fees invoice may need to know the number of modules or their subject before the precise fee can be determined. This may affect part-time students more than full-time students, if the part-time fee is determined purely by the modules taken rather than on a notional course fee.

2.12 Induction

Enrolment is for the institution, induction is for the student. Both needs are important, but keeping the balance is not always easy. Induction covers several areas:

- induction to the course and modules, local safety requirements (the academic department);
- induction to the institution and its facilities, library, careers, counsellors, etc. (the centre and the support departments);
- induction to social and leisure facilities (the students union).

Some new students enjoy their induction to the institution, others find it a distraction from their eagerness to get on with the studies for which they have so keenly enrolled. In both cases, it is important not to overload the students with information: the key approach is usually to ensure that the students obtain enough detail to know where to go for fuller information. Too much detail, whether on academic or on non-academic matters, right at the start of the course can lead to so-called 'induction fatigue', and a lack of attention to what is being said that completely undermines the aims of the exercise.

If a student handbook is issued, it should be kept fairly friendly. The student handbook is not a substitute for induction, but it can be an indispensable adjunct. There is a need to ensure that students receive the formal regulations which they need (see Chapter 8, section 8.8), but in most cases this can be done by a mention of the key features and a reference to the main regulations document, be it in the library or on-line. However, it is very important not to paraphrase or summarize the full regulations in a way which inadvertently changes the sense or omits key features, as even a slightly different interpretation could be legally binding if it is all the student has been given and if the student has good reason to treat it as authoritative.

Induction on social and leisure facilities is often managed by the students themselves (e.g. through the students union), especially in relation to societies and entertainments. The institution may also take the opportunity to permit outside agencies to make presentations on services which they wish to offer to students: banks, travel services, insurance, shops and the inevitable poster sales.

In many institutions the head of the institution (vice-chancellor, principal etc.) may also wish to address the new students, which can present interesting challenges in finding enough large rooms and times in the induction schedule to fit them.

The hardest part is to stop each individual aspect from dominating the induction: keep each contributor to strict time and volume limits. This can call for great tact on the part of the organizer.

2.13 The changing role of personal care ■

The concept of personal or pastoral care of students has undergone many changes in the history of further and higher education. With its roots in the *in loco parentis* role of the private school or college, it has developed through the personal tutor, whose main duty was the protection of the morals of the student, into a large-scale combination of social work, counselling and provision of ancillary services (see Bell 1996; Rowley 1996).

The range of services provided to look after the personal needs of students is large and varied: in many institutions the student can find every amenity that could be expected in a small town or large village: careers, doctors, dentists, childcare, crèche, catering, financial guidance, religious services and counselling, accommodation etc. In many of these the service offered to the student is essentially the same as that which a similar facility would offer in any large community: the main distinctive issue connected with offering the services to students is that the students can be a transient population, and one which is only at the institution for about two-thirds of the year. The counselling services also have the special stress of a large number of novice students at the start of the course, who suffer either severe homesickness or acute euphoria at having left home. Apart from this factor, shared to a greater or lesser extent by the other pastoral care sectors, the role and approach of the support staff is governed less by the traditions of education than by the prevailing practices of their colleagues outside education.

The rise of counselling and support services in the 1980s was followed by a levelling off, and in some cases a contraction, as concern arose that ever more resources were being spent on supporting students in the stressful atmosphere of mass education, which could be spent more effectively on teaching and learning facilities to remove the stress in the first place.

2.14   Who can offer advice to students?

In addition to the trained and skilled counsellors referred to in section 2.13, most students have a very wide range of knowledgeable staff in the institution to whom they can turn for help on personal as well as academic matters. Not only their personal and subject tutors, but also the students union and relevant administrators in their academic department or in the central administration (though the latter still seem to engender a certain amount of trepidation on the part of students), can offer valid advice to students within their own areas of expertise and competence, and students must be encouraged to approach them freely and openly.

The student administration sections (whether central or departmental) have their main strength in advising students on regulatory matters, as regards both internal regulations and external legislation. When it is a question of helping students to choose the right modules to fit their course or their career plans, the main areas of expertise usually reside with the academic staff, although there are certainly admirable examples of professional course counsellors being located within the support service department. This is closely allied to careers advice, which is similarly equally well approached by academic tutors within the student's department as by professional careers advisors. The need for tutorial advice in module choice is examined further in Chapter 3, with regard to course construction.

2.15   Catching personal problems

Although students are deemed, in the eyes of the law, to be independent adults by the time they are in higher education, and responsible for most of their own decisions when they are in further or higher education, most institutions still feel that they owe it to the students in their care to keep an eye open for imminent or latent problems. As mass education has led to reduced personal contact between tutors and students, it is less easy for staff to spot gradual changes in student behaviour. Chapter 7 (on records) explores the way in which attendance monitoring (active or passive) can be used as one means of noting when students may be having academic or personal problems. This cannot be used as a total substitute for encouraging students to bring their problems voluntarily to their tutors before they become major issues.

2.16   Pastoral care in examinations ■

One of the main areas in which all parts of the institution can offer real help to students is in the provision of special examination facilities for students with short-term or long-term disabilities. Here the institution is showing that it can be flexible within its regulations and procedures so as to ensure that all the students are being assessed on a comparable basis. This is discussed in greater depth in Chapter 4 (section 4.5).

2.17   Pastoral care of part-time and evening students ■

Students attending courses at an institution deserve the same level of support and personal care irrespective of when they are attending. In institutions where the majority of students attend during the day (either as full-time students or as daytime part-time students), there can be significant challenges in living up to this expectation for students who attend in the evenings. This is particularly the case where the numbers are relatively small, and can make some provisions potentially unviable in economic terms. Nevertheless, if the institution is committed equally to all of its students it should ensure that good provision is available at all times: catering, leisure space, library and computing facilities can be difficult to provide if numbers are small or located in scattered locations throughout the institution, but are usually readily identified as being worth providing, particularly if many of the students are coming direct from work for the evening classes and need to have a meal or relaxation before starting their studies.

Less commonly available are the non-pastoral student support areas such as registry and finance, except at enrolment. This can make it difficult for evening students to get questions answered as easily as other students if the staff who know the particular answers only work during the day. In more traditional evening attendance courses it is quite common for the students, often with rival domestic commitments, not to place too high demands on ancillary services. With the spread of mixed-mode attendance this cannot be assumed, and there is a very good case for all the facilities and administrations to be opened until mid or late evening, with key facilities such as library and computing to be open for approaching 24 hours, if the evening students are not to feel like second-class citizens. In some areas the institution may have to subsidize or provide transport to residential areas so that students can attend at times governed by the needs of the course rather than at the whim of the local transport agency.

2.18 Support for students with disabilities

As well as the support during examinations mentioned in section 2.16 above and in Chapter 4, institutions need to be highly aware of the need to ensure easy access to all their facilities. There is much more to this than simply considering wheelchair access. Suffice it to say here that finding a good solution for these issues can benefit the whole institution: it is not just students with disabilities who benefit from automatic doors and the removal of steps, but also delivery staff, parents with children, any person carrying difficult loads (files, computers, books, etc.), and, of course, the institution's staff in general. If the institution has ensured that there is wheelchair access to all its buildings, the provision of a special version of the campus map showing the recommended routes and access points can be invaluable for a great many purposes.

However, the full scope of a discussion on how these needs can best be addressed is far beyond the scope of this book, as it needs to take into account not just student administration, but also building works, legislation on health and safety and, last but not least, public relations (see Palfreyman and Warner 1998: Chapter 19).

2.19 The role of alumni associations

The tradition of 'alumni' associations or 'graduates' associations is long. In some countries it has a more active tradition than in others.

The roles of such associations are varied, and range from the simple 'old chums club' through to a vigorous fund-raising body. These roles are not incompatible. Fundamental to all such activities is a need to keep the loyalty and interest of former students; the best way of doing this is by maintaining regular contact with news items of relevant interest to them. This includes not just updates on the lives of their fellow former students but also features on what is happening to the institution since they have left. The motives of the readers vary from simply keeping in touch with (or about) people they knew, to an active participation in promoting the development of their former institution. There is no relative merit value attached to either of these approaches: both are symptoms of a healthy institution.

The institution may decide that it wants to encourage one of the above models rather than the other, or to encourage both within the same association. There is no inconsistency between organizing an annual or quinquennial reunion on one hand, and marketing and fund-raising at the other extreme, including promotions of services from outside commercial agencies (insurance discounts, travel clubs, credit cards, etc.), although it must be borne in mind that some people resent over-persistent marketing tactics and feel that it suggests that the institution only values them as a sales opportunity rather than as a member of the larger institutional community.

2.20 For whose benefit is the alumni association? ■

If the contrasting (but not conflicting) approaches are handled well all parties benefit from the exercise. The institution gains a body of supporters who, actively or imperceptibly, support their old institution to others; the former scholars gain a feeling that their institution really valued their presence, which in turn makes them feel that they acted wisely in choosing such a caring institution at which to study. No graduates would like to have taken a course at an institution which subsequently becomes regarded as failing; if they can help to perpetuate the prosperity and good reputation of their former institution then both parties benefit. One activity in which both the institution and its association can participate for the benefit of others arises when hardship funds or scholarships are set up, funded by either or by both.

2.21 Who are the alumni associations for? ■

In a literal sense, a 'graduates association' ought only to be for 'graduates', i.e. those with 'degrees' (see Chapter 5). An 'alumni association' means just 'association of pupils' and can therefore more clearly include all students who have completed a course of any sort; however, this Latin term has overtones of traditional universities with which many institutions do not wish to feel associated. Fortunately, the literal meaning of the terms is not usually felt to constrain the actual membership, and 'graduates' associations often include those who took certificates, diplomas or even non-award courses.

Having decided whether its association is just for graduates or for all former scholars, the institution must be clear whether it is also open not only to those who successfully completed their course but to any student who attended even just part of a course. It may be felt to be elitist to restrict membership to those who successfully completed a course, and may denigrate the feelings of those who, for a variety of reasons, were unable to leave with a qualification.

Not many institutions, on the other hand, would extend membership to those who merely attended short courses or took individual modules as associate students or extramural courses. There is no right or wrong on this: each institution can, and should, decide its own policy in line with its view of its role in society.

2.22 Making use of alumni

Apart from simple marketing activities, an institution can benefit from its links with former students in many ways as part of its general promotion. Keeping in touch with former students can help the institution to identify those who have reached positions of influence, and use these contacts for the benefit of the institution. Such promotion is not just to be seen as a political or financial activity. Keeping active contact with employers and managers can help to foster industrial links, which in turn can provide valuable opportunities for work experience for the next generations of students.

2.23 Who runs the alumni association?

There is no 'correct' model for this, and it is closely linked with the role which the institution has decided for its association, and the intensity of its activities. Some associations are run entirely by the institution itself, sometimes linked with the public relations department; others are run by the former scholars themselves for the mutual good.

2.24 Are alumni associations a good thing?

Undoubtedly yes. An institution without an alumni association is weakened by its lack of links with the activities of its former students. It could end up with no real idea of how it is perceived and, more importantly, represented by those who have had the most intimate experience of the institution itself.

3

COURSE CONSTRUCTION AND MODULE CHOICE

Whether it matters how a course is constructed, and how courses should be managed for the benefit of students.

Take thou what course thou wilt.
> (William Shakespeare, *Julius Caesar*, III.ii.266)

I only took the regular course.
> (Lewis Carroll, *Alice's Adventures in Wonderland*, Chapter 9)

3.1 The need for management of courses

The construction of courses has changed quite dramatically since the 1970s. Until then most courses were fairly traditional in their construction: three years of study on a wide ranging but fairly static syllabus with a set of traditional written examinations at the end of the course. Apart from choosing an area of specialization, or a topic for a project, there were relatively few possibilities for options in the sense of unrestricted free choices. From the academic point of view, 'management' of the course consisted in little more than updating the syllabus for the latest developments.

The explosion of variant courses since then, along with the introduction of modular courses, has added considerably to the complexity of course management. Under the more traditional structure it was sufficient to define a course, record that a student was on that course and wait until they took their examinations. Although this change has great implications for record keeping (see Chapter 7), it has also meant that the concept of 'course construction' has had to become a more active exercise.

The arrival of non-standard courses has also tested the traditional concepts of course management as well as record keeping. Courses can be offered as full-time, part-time, thin sandwich, thick sandwich, day release, block release, extended year; 'short–fat', 'long–thin'; multiple cohort, dual intake; calendar year or academic year; undergraduate, enhanced undergraduate, sub-degree, postgraduate, in-service, pre-registration, post-registration, post-experience, professional update; taught, research; internal, external, franchised, validated, distance-learning, work-based; vocational; open-learning, computer-based learning, portfolio-based; and so on. The ingenuity shown in finding new methods of course delivery, in a desire to find and tap new market niches, is enormous, and still probably far from exhausted. It would be tempting to fear that the system might seize up under its own complexity, were it not for the suspicion that these fears have been present ever since the first universities were founded and have so far not proved insurmountable.

It is up to the academic management to decide which structure to adopt for a particular course: the administrative implications often come as a secondary consideration. Mostly, however, it can be summarized as 'ever more detail'. The pedagogic strengths and weaknesses of the various models will not be discussed in this book.

To some institutions the growth of extended courses, to which they may be less accustomed, can present particular problems. These are situations where a student's study can be spread over a relatively indeterminate number of years, with some parts of the course taken one year, then perhaps a year off, then some more parts of the course and so on. Often described as 'lifelong learning', it is not a new phenomenon, and has an extensive history in schemes for continuous professional updating and 'in-service' courses. This structure can present novel planning methods for course construction, particularly in defining how long the maximum period of study is before the earlier topics are no longer deemed up to date for the final award. There are more intricate problems, however, in managing the course and its students once it is running, which are covered in Chapter 7 (section 7.3).

3.2 What is a course?

A course is often no longer a course, at least in modular structures: it is the amalgam of the various modules which the student has chosen from those available, with the intention of making an interesting and academically viable overall theme. Non-modular courses, even those with a choice of specialization, do not present many novel administrative features compared to the traditional course described in section 3.1 above.

Modular schemes vary: there is no standard model for modularization. The differences may be summarized as three stages of freedom.

Unitization

Unitization is often just a cosmetic reconfiguration of the traditional degree described above, and a nod in the direction of modularization. Typically it consists of little more than ensuring that as many courses as possible are based on a common credit currency; it does not require that all course components are the same size, or even compatible sizes, or that all courses have the same overall workload. As long as courses are self-contained, it matters little if some work on credit points, some on percentages and some on modules/units; as students are given increasing scope for picking options from other courses this makes calculation of results and classifications increasingly challenging. Unitization is, however, a prerequisite for higher levels of modularization.

Management of students on such courses is along relatively traditional lines. It is known from the start what awards and course titles the students are aiming for, and if they fail to meet the defined criteria they may find themselves leaving without an award.

Modular framework

A 'modular framework' is the next stage towards full modularization. In such schemes there will typically be an overall single model of course construction: so many modules, each of such and such a value, standard criteria for progression, a standard formula for classification etc. However, the courses will normally all be quite closely defined, and in some cases may be completely determined with no options or any other flexibility. Management of students on these courses is still largely along traditional lines, and has the same concept of course criteria as mentioned for the 'unitized' courses above.

Modular scheme

Most radical are the fully fledged 'modular schemes', often rather disparagingly described as 'pick and mix' courses. In the most absolute of these even the concept of 'course title' may be more difficult to pin down: in some the final year board of examiners considers the modules passed by the student and determines which of a range of awards the student may be qualified for; in others the course title may be indeterminate and is really more a description of the subjects studied by the individual student (e.g. 'BA in French, Law and Sociology'). In such schemes there may be little or no constraint on the course titles available to the board of examiners, and the prospectus entry may contain a single, large entry for a course title such as 'BA Combined Studies' plus a provision for a subtitle such as 'majoring in X'. Management of students on such schemes is module-driven: there may be little concept of 'course' until the final board of examiners (although there may be 'pathways'); nor need there be 'course transfers' to process. What does increase is the responsibility for advising the students through what can appear an amorphous jumble of unrelated subjects.

3.3 Management of options

The concept of 'specialist subjects' is reasonably well established; relatively more recent is the spread of unconstrained 'free choice' subjects, also known as 'electives'. Driven essentially by a desire to avoid over-specialization and to broaden a student's knowledge base, and encourage transferable (and marketable) skills such as numeracy, information technology and languages, they add a level of complexity not to the construction of courses themselves but to the management of the students and their choices.

It is up to the institution to decide how many such free choice subjects it allows on each course on pedagogic grounds; in fact in some institutions the taking of such subjects is compulsory to the extent that they must be taken in subjects totally unrelated to the core subject of the student's course. Care must be taken to ensure that the regulations are clear on what happens to students if they fail compulsory free choice subjects, and that the students understand the implications of this. If the boards of examiners always ignore or condone failure in free choice modules there seems little incentive for students to bother taking them; it also causes resentment on the part of the tutors of such modules, who feel that their subject is not being taken seriously.

One of the immediate problems in managing students' free choices, or, indeed, options of any sort, is finding out which modules the student is taking. It is common practice for students to be given a week or so at the start of the teaching period in which they can try modules to see if they like them before confirming their actual choice. The extent to which this is allowed (how many can be tried, how long before the choice is confirmed) is an academic matter: the administrative load is the same, and consists mainly in convincing students that it is important that the records on their module choice are updated.

In terms of management of non-student matters, the main implications of this flexibility are that it makes it virtually impossible to compile a teaching timetable, to carry out precise forward planning of supply and demand and even to calculate the teaching resources to be allocated to the academic department in time for the start of the budgetary period. Some institutions try to get round these problems by carrying out a provisional registration of modules in the preceding year/semester; this may be of some value but is limited by the extent to which students are bound by their provisional choice.

The more flexibility offered to students, the greater the onus on the institution to help students to make a rational choice of subjects on their courses. Such advice can be in paper form, on-line or face-to-face. The last is very resource intensive but very flexible: paper-based or on-line guidance can be much more detailed (and should in any case also be available if there is personal counselling), but it carries with it a continuous responsibility for ensuring that the data are correct and up to date. This can be an intensive activity, but is vital. It is also important that the institution decides (and the students understand) who bears the responsibility if the student makes an inappropriate choice, despite the counselling offered.

3.4 Student involvement

The idea of involving students in the construction and development of their own courses is relatively new. Although not unique to education, it is one of the features which makes the relationship of the student to the institution that of 'client' or 'consumer' rather than 'customer' (see Chapter 8, section 8.5). There are two quite well established ways of doing this: questionnaires and committees. Consulting students via questionnaires to find out which parts of their studies are not working in the way they would like has, in some cases, reached epidemic proportions, and has sometimes contributed to what has been termed 'questionnaire fatigue'. This can be a real phenomenon if students receive separate questionnaires on each aspect of their course – module, course, library, computing, support, etc. – and the reluctance to supply meaningful responses is even greater if the students feel that nothing is likely to be changed as a result of the survey. There is also a real point that student responses to module questionnaires do not change things for the students who are completing them: at best they are contributing to improvements for the next cohort of students, a level of philanthropy and altruism which may test the enthusiasm of hard-pressed respondents (see Harvey 1997).

A more direct way of involving students, and the most useful for tackling current problems, is the 'course committee'. Ideally this should consist of all the tutors on the course, with enough student representatives to make sure that they cannot be overwhelmed. It matters little how the students gain membership of the committee, provided they understand that they are there to represent the views of all the students on the course, not just their own, and that they communicate with those whom they represent. These committees can be extremely effective at dealing with niggles before they become major issues, but, as with questionnaires, their effectiveness is severely undermined if the students feel that they are just a toothless talking shop, or a sop to democracy: it is vital that students (direct or via the committee) are given prompt feedback on all issues which they raise, even if it is not the solution that they sought.

3.5 Course approval

Methods of approving courses are very varied, inclined to follow fashion and to be guided by what external bodies signal as being good models. The strengths and weaknesses of the models will not be discussed here, only the implications for student administration.

The key factor in approving courses, in order to minimize future disruption to students, is to ensure that all the details of the course are clearly agreed when the documents are approved. There must be a clear, comprehensive yet concise and intelligible course document in which students can find out everything they need to know. But brevity should not be sought by summarising the full institutional regulations – any discrepancy can cause great problems if there is a judicial review about any alleged misapplication of the rules (see Chapter 8, section 8.12).

Similarly, but more indirectly, there must be no loose ends in the course structure which might have to be sorted out later in a way which changes what is offered to the students. For example, the institution must be absolutely clear exactly how the course will figure in all its statutory returns. This is not always as straightforward as it seems, if funding agencies insist on classifying courses in a way which has not kept pace with rapidly evolving modes of study: for example, do 'post-experience' courses count as 'undergraduate' or 'postgraduate'? It is no good discovering at the time of the first statistical return that a wrong assumption about the way in which a particular award or mode of attendance will be reported will cause incompatibilities and reduced government funding: by that stage the students will insist that the course as originally offered to them must continue.

If the institution approves its courses for a fixed period, followed by a periodic review for the next period, the use of student views at the time of course review is as vital as it is during the operation of the course. A review panel should seek the views of the students at present on the course, preferably face-to-face rather than via questionnaires; this can be a useful test of the openness of any critical review submitted by the course team as part of the review. This too enhances the perception of the student population that their views are not only sought but listened to.

3.6 Course changes ▮

In Chapter 8 (section 8.8) there is a brief discussion on whether a course can be changed while the students are on it. Very often, no matter what the formal legal position, students can be persuaded that a change is beneficial to them, or at least justifiable in removing anomalies. Course changes can therefore happen during the period of validity of the syllabus, although obviously it will reduce student confidence in the management if this happens too often.

3.7 External factors ▮

Chapter 8 (section 8.9) also touches on the influence of external agencies on course construction. This concerns not just the requirements of professional bodies, but also the views (and what are perceived as the preferred models) of statutory quality agencies and visits from funding councils and governmental regulatory bodies.

4

EXAMINATIONS

How to know what students are doing, keep it painless for them from beginning to end, and how to constrain cheating.

Make that thy question, and go rot!
(William Shakespeare, *The Winter's Tale*, I.ii.324)

4.1 The change in assessment methods

The management of examinations is hugely complex. It was not always so. The traditional method of assessing a student's knowledge of the subject was by means of formal invigilated written examinations taken at the end of the course; in some cases there might also have been examinations at the end of earlier years, but these were often only for secondary subjects, or were nearer to progress reports (though termination of enrolment could still be the outcome of failure). Practical subjects also had laboratory examinations.

This chapter does not assess the relative pedagogic merits of the different ways of assessing students (see Ramsden 1992, concerning 'shallow/surface learning' and 'deep learning' as influenced by assessment methods, and likewise CSUP 1992):

- invigilated written examinations;
- essays;
- paper-based or computerized multiple-choice papers (often referred to by students as 'multiple-guess' papers);
- other forms of computerized tests;
- 'seen' papers issued in advance;
- 'take-away' examinations;
- 'open book' papers, whether 'restricted' (specified texts only) or 'unrestricted' (take in anything you like);
- portfolios;

- oral examinations (not just for languages);
- orally defended thesis;
- open-ended examinations with no time limit (an experiment in the 1960s, though not widely in use);
- group assessment;
- peer assessment;
- or any other of the wide variety of methods (the choice of these should depend on an academic judgement of which method best assesses whatever it is that is to be measured).

There are administrative implications for all of the above, but that ought to be a secondary factor in deciding the method – albeit an important one. In some cases the academic ideal may have to be compromised on grounds of manageability. For example, overuse of essays leads to very complex procedures for the collection of interim marks and measures to record and verify submission (not to mention avoiding clumping of deadlines); extensive use of written examinations on courses with many opportunities for options can lead to intractable timetabling problems; using too many different assessment methods can increase the complexity of the mark sheets (whether on paper or on-line), of transcripts and results letters and of information on resits and progression.

The notes below concentrate on formal, timed, invigilated, written examinations, and on essay-style coursework. Similarly, there is no discussion on the arguments as to whether there should be resit examinations, when they should be, and whether there should be a penalty attached to it being a resit (maximum mark, etc.); these are pedagogic matters and practice varies widely as a matter of local taste and convention.

4.2 Examination timetable

In the sort of courses which were standard at higher education institutions until the rise of modularization and the spread of 'free choice' subjects, it was relatively easy to compile the examination timetable: the main constraint was fitting the students into the available accommodation. It was not at all uncommon to find that the same examination timetable was used for many years in succession, to the extent that for some courses with very stable or highly prescribed content the examination timetable was published in the institution's calendar several years in advance.

Two factors have disturbed this stability: the increasing flexibility of courses and the huge increase in student numbers. The former has created many more potential clashes in the examination time-table, making it spread over a greater length of time; the latter has often outstripped the supply of available suitable accommodation, also making the timetable spread over a longer period. Over-reliance on publicly booked halls for examinations can make the institution very vulnerable to competing bookings, and to different priorities for the owners of the halls: sports halls may wish to be hosts to prestigious competitions and feel that this is a higher priority than student examinations; the accommodation may disappear completely for redevelopment at very short notice. Increasing hiring costs must also be allowed for. It is very wise to draw up an inventory of emergency accommodation (drawing offices, gymnasia, halls belonging to nearby religious organizations, etc.) which is not suitable for regular use but would be acceptable in an emergency. There are two situations to cover: a room becoming unavailable when compiling the examination timetable (e.g. when a booking is turned down), and a room becoming unavailable in the middle of the examination period (e.g. following a fire). If there is a neighbouring institution which has a different examination profile this can be an excellent opportunity for mutual emergency cover.

The increased complexity of clashes is not just a function of the rise in the number of free choice options and joint degrees: it can also be caused by attempts made, in the interests of economy, to use individual modules on a wider variety of courses, rather than having minor variants tailored to individual courses. This means not only that the number of candidates on individual modules can be very large (figures well in excess of 500 are fairly frequent), but also that these modules tend to clash with every other module on the examination timetable. Large modules also produce requests from the beleaguered markers to have the examination in an early slot in the timetable, simply as a means of ensuring sufficient time for marking.

To some extent these pressures have been moderated by the growth in assessment by coursework, but this cannot be taken as a reliable solution since there are also pressures to move back from coursework to invigilated examinations as a remedy for remorselessly increasing tutor workload. Similarly changes in teaching and learning methods may reduce the number of large flat classrooms for use in examinations as methods move to more 'student-centred' approaches, and large formal rooms become converted into work areas or computer laboratories (often without the examination administrators being informed). Tiered rooms are not normally suitable for examinations, because of the ease with which candidates on the higher tiers can see the work of the others; if the room has continuous benches rather than movable seats it not only increases the ease of passing notes between students but also makes it difficulty for the invigil-ators to move around the candidates. Avoiding this can mean that a tiered lecture theatre of capacity 200 may only have a usable capa-city in examination conditions of about 50 (widely spaced, alternate rows, etc.).

As the standard academic year has not been lengthened, the extension of the examinations period to cope with larger numbers has had to overflow at one end or the other: either the examination period starts earlier and encroaches on teaching time, or it overflows into the 'marking' period at the end of term.

When all the potential clashes and accommodation constraints have been identified, there are many other factors which an institu-tion may wish to take into account in the examination timetable:

(a) Part-time students will have work and domestic commitments outside their studies; it may not be possible to guarantee to fit around these, especially if there are large numbers of them, but the institution may wish to try to publish the examination time-table many months in advance so that the part-time students can arrange their commitments around them. In particular, it must be clearly understood by students and by the institution whether the fact that a course is taught in the evening or on a particular day implies that any examinations will be on the same evening or day. In many cases this simply cannot be guaranteed: for example, if a particular module is taught separately to daytime and evening students but has to have a common examination. This may be seen as poor 'customer care' by some students.

(b) Part-time students on courses which also have full-time modes often follow more flexible study patterns than their full-time colleagues: they may take modules in a different order, or be permitted to trail modules from one stage to the next. This can create strange combinations and intractable clashes for the exam-ination timetable.

(c) If the course is offered in partnership between two institutions (for example, in a franchising agreement), the examination time-table of the parent institution must take into account the local needs of students at the partner colleges, where the examination is taken in parallel at each institution. For example, the parent institution must not assume that late afternoon, evening or week-end examinations are equally easy for the partner colleges in terms of accommodation, invigilation, access, transport or catering.

(d) Even more complex are cases where a course is also taught at a partner college outside the country in which the parent insti-tution is situated. As well as the considerations in (c) above the timetable must take account of the need to hold examinations simultaneously. If only one foreign time zone is involved it may be possible, for example, to hold an examination in the morning in one centre at the same time as it is being taken in the late afternoon in the other country (for example, in the United Kingdom and the Far East). If the time zones are too far apart it may be necessary to require separate examinations, with all the problems which that raises about comparability (and workload for question setters). Absolute simultaneity is not vital provided that the examinations overlap, and that no one leaves the early sitting before the later one has started, or starts the later session after candidates have finished the earlier one: this may involve suspension of any rules which normally allow students to start late or leave early.

(e) Similar points to those in (d) can arise even where there are no parallel offerings of the course in other countries: the institution may, on compassionate grounds, permit a student to take an examination in their own country (see Chapter 8, section 8.6(d)). The management of examinations taken away from the main centre is considered further in section 4.15.

(f) Many students have constraints placed upon their attendance for examinations by their religious observances: this may involve not being available at particular times of the day, on particular days of the week or in particular weeks of the year. It is definitely best to require students to inform the institution of any such constraints before the examination timetable is compiled, not to wait until it is published and then ask for changes whose resolution may require the recompilation of the whole timetable. It is also prudent to require confirmation from the students' local religious leader that the constraint is legitimate, as otherwise there is an open invitation for students to place frivolous requests merely for social reasons. Examinations officers will be familiar with requests from students to avoid putting their examinations near departmental party days, or when the local sports team is playing at home, and there should be no incentive for students to claim bogus religious affiliations merely to ensure that their examinations do not clash with social activities. There can still be no absolute guarantees that these religious requirements can be accommodated, and 'chaperoning' may be required, as mentioned under (k) below. It is possible to get lists of all the principal religious festivals from charitable agencies, from books of dates and from on-line electronic sources.

(g) Examiners have many pressures on their time. This does not excuse the frequent requests which are submitted asking that their examination should be on (or should avoid) a particular day so as to avoid their holiday commitments. This is unreasonable.

(h) Students (and many staff) cherish a belief that they can complain if their examinations are too close together, though others complain if they are too spread out. The institution must make clear its policy on this. With very complex examination timetables it is virtually impossible to guarantee that students will not have two examinations on the same day, or more than five in a single week.

(i) Considerations such as the avoidance of 'examination bunching' described in (h) lead to one of the main tensions in publishing the examination timetable. Most administrators responsible for compiling the timetable will recognize the feeling that they could have produced a better timetable if they had had more time: there is always a conflict between early publication of the timetable and optimisation of the distribution of examinations and the utilization of accommodation and invigilators.

(j) Is there a computer algorithm to produce the timetable? Unfortunately not. There are some excellent pieces of software available which will *probably* produce a workable timetable, whether it is a teaching timetable or an examination timetable, but these cannot guarantee a solution, particularly if there are many constraints on clashes or accommodation. It has been mathematically proved that there cannot be a computer algorithm to provide a solution. This does not, of course, mean that a solution will not manifest itself in most cases, it is just that this cannot be guaranteed. Nor does this stop students, as part of their projects, attempting to find novel algorithms for producing a faultless timetable which meets all the constraints.

(k) Sometimes, despite all the efforts of those compiling the examination timetable, there remain totally intractable clashes. Given unlimited accommodation, and no restriction on the length of the examination period or the use of evenings, Saturdays and Sundays, there should be no clashes, but this cannot be guaranteed. The institution must have a policy for dealing with the students involved: setting variant examinations is undesirable, and the normal solution is to let the student take the examination in the session immediately before or after the main one, with the student being chaperoned between sessions to ensure no leakage of questions; this may involve an overnight supervision. The onus of providing the chaperone should reside with the academic department responsible for that student: it is part of pastoral tutorial care.

4.3 Management of the examination centres

The administrator's first task, once the examination accommodation has been identified as part of the timetabling, is to ensure that there are sufficient invigilators. If the ratio of invigilators to candidates is correct there are relatively few differences between managing large and small rooms, and it is up to the institution to determine its pattern of accommodation in the light of what is available: large rooms may need microphones for the announcements and may have congestion problems at the start and end, but they reduce the risk of students going to the wrong place; small rooms may reduce the complexity of managing examinations of varying lengths but increase the complexity of packing the materials.

The most common ratio of invigilators to students is about 1:50, though some have as many as 1:40 and some as few as 1:60. There are some economies of scale, particularly if, as is prudent, a minimum of two invigilators must be assigned to each room (to ensure coverage if one has to leave). This means that using small rooms can be very expensive in invigilation, as there may be a need to have two invigilators in rooms with only 20–50 candidates, which is a ratio of 1:25 or less. Three hundred students spread around six 50-seater rooms may therefore require 12 invigilators, whereas one large 300-seater room can manage the same number of students with only six invigilators.

Particularly in larger rooms, or any room where there are more than three invigilators, it is worth considering designating one of them as 'chief invigilator'. This ensures that one person is acknowledged to be the person in charge in case decisions need to be made, reducing the risk of the co-invigilators disagreeing about the apportionment of duties. It is best if the chief invigilators can be appointed in advance by the examinations office or registry, rather than decided 'by mutual agreement' on the day, as that can lead to tensions. Some academic staff are born organizers and enjoy being chief invigilators; some do not. It is best to choose those who do, unless there is particular reason for wishing to improve the expertise of the others.

Practices vary from one institution to another about whether invigilators are chosen from academic staff or from a pool of external specialists. There are strengths in both methods. Using externals costs more but their attitude is more easily controlled; using academic staff is cheaper and gives a guaranteed pool of invigilators but does not equally guarantee that their heart will be in the task. Spouses of academic staff have often been used as invigilators, but this appears to be a diminishing pool of availability. The use of research students is quite common, and can give relief to hard-pressed academic staff, but care must be taken that the students are not inadvertently given supervision of their friends.

It does not really matter where the invigilators sit, provided that they can see the candidates, that the candidates can see them and that the invigilators can easily get to the candidates if the need arises. It is good practice in larger rooms to put one or more of the invigilators at the back and sides of the room, first to enable speedier access to students who need help, but also to keep a closer eye on candidates who would otherwise be rather distant from the invigilators' seats.

It is very tempting for busy academic staff who have been given invigilation duties to use the time in a way which they feel is more productive. This must be discouraged: invigilation is a full-time occupation, and those in charge should not be permitted to take marking with them, to read, to use portable computers or (as has happened on more than one occasion) to fall asleep or to watch portable televisions (particularly when tennis or cricket competitions are being shown).

A contentious aspect of examinations which can easily be overlooked is the security of candidates' materials which they are required to leave outside the room. It is uncommon for there to be a convenient room in which to leave coats, bags, umbrellas, notebooks, etc., and even rarer for the institution to be able to supervise the area. It should be made clear to students that they leave such materials unsupervised entirely at their own risk, and that the institution cannot indemnify them against theft or loss, any more than in any other part of the institution.

One of the hardest things to manage in examination rooms, and fortunately quite rare, is the procedure for fire alarms and bomb alerts. In themselves they present few problems about evacuation, as the procedures for this should have been established already for other uses of the rooms. The particular problem is to stop the candidates from talking to each other during the evacuation. If this happens the candidates *must* be reported for cheating; in extreme cases the examination itself must be cancelled. This must also be considered if the period of evacuation is long or disruptive. It is an unfortunate fact that some of the alarms are set off deliberately as a means of cheating – a candidate arranges for a friend to set off the alarm so that during the evacuation the questions can be looked up in notes or discussed with other candidates. If the examination is cancelled a replacement must be set, and held within a short period of time. Again there are unfortunate examples where a policy of simply using an existing coursework mark instead of setting a new examination has led some students, knowing that they have good coursework marks and that they do not perform well in examinations, to arrange deliberately for the fire alarms to be set off so that the examination will be declared void. To avoid this abuse, a replacement examination *must* be arranged.

A more common disruption is that caused by students arriving too late, or wishing to leave early. Were it not for the possibility of cheating there is little intrinsic reason for barring either of these. The main purpose in trying to stop students leaving early is to try to stop them from giving in to that panic feeling which many feel on first reading of the question paper: typically institutions forbid candidates from leaving in the first 30 minutes of the examination. This cushion also means that invigilators can admit late candidates during the same period: if no one has left, there can be no chance of anyone having passed on the questions to a student waiting to do a little 'quick revision' before entering. If any candidate has left, no other candidates should be permitted to enter late, even if on a different examination (there have been cases where students, on leaving, have picked up the question paper from the desk of a colleague on a different examination who was waiting outside and about to enter). A student who arrives too late to be admitted should be referred to either their tutor or the examinations office, according to local rules. It is up to the institution to formulate clear procedures for handling such cases, but a fundamental rule should be that any time missed by arriving late is not added on the end as compensation; doing so gives an unfair advantage compared to students who have rushed to the examination centre in order to arrive on time. Students who miss the examination altogether may, if the institution so wishes, be permitted to take the examination under special invigilation, but there should be no guarantee that it will be marked or that any mark will be accepted; any such case must be reported to the board of examiners as 'suspect'.

One of the most tedious tasks for the invigilators is the monitoring of examination materials, not only those provided by the institution but also those which students wish to bring into the room. Materials required for the examination should have been sorted out in advance and already be in the room. The main complication arises with 'open book examinations' where the examiner has not made it clear what this phrase means – it can mean 'a clean copy of a specified text', or 'anything that the student wishes to bring in'; typically it should exclude library books (whether from the institution's library or from any other) as that would give unfair advantage to the first student who could reach the library and borrow the book. Phrases such as 'without notes' should be avoided, as students may not be clear whether this means 'an unannotated edition' without any editorial notes by the publisher, or 'without having any personal notes added by the student': candidates may realize that the latter could be cheating but not realize that the former is also excluded.

The main problem is with all the small items which students wish to bring with them. Unfortunately, however sympathetic the invigilators may wish to appear, the granting of maximum flexibility will be abused by those candidates who wish to cheat:

- lucky mascots can have notes hidden in them;
- dictionaries can conceal notes or crib sheets;
- calculators can contain notes in their memory or instruction booklets, or tucked into the carrying case;
- pencil cases can have notes written on the inside;
- personal scrap paper and other stationery can have notes concealed in them or in some cases can have prepared answers for attaching to the submitted script as if they had just been written;
- correcting fluid can have notes written inside the wrapper;
- mobile phones can be used during toilet trips;
- earphones and tapes of notes may be masquerading as hearing aids.

The only solution is eternal vigilance, a suspicious mind and a rigorous implementation of the regulations. If dictionaries are permitted they should be provided by the institution or their use should be permitted merely for the first 15 minutes, so that unknown words can be checked by students whose mother tongue is different, but without giving a potential advantage to students who keep the dictionary throughout the examination; if students are permitted to use their own copies the institution must consider defining acceptable editions, since some 'dictionaries' are nearer to being reference books, even if bilingual.

Similar considerations apply to calculators: either a standard model should be made available or defined, or each machine will have to be checked individually, which also involves clearing any memories which it might have, particularly text memory. The difference between calculators and computers is not easy to define, and vigilant students may exploit any ill-phrased definitions and try to bring in laptop or palmtop computers on the grounds that they are 'calculators' or contain a 'dictionary'.

If the invigilator suspects any misuse of materials, dictionaries or calculators, the items in question must be confiscated and reported under the cheating regulations. Invigilators should resist the temptation to judge the matters locally, since this can lead to great inconsistency between examinations, and confusion for students if materials tolerated in one session are suddenly alleged to be being used for cheating in another session. (See also section 4.13 on cheating.)

4.4   Migrating desk syndrome

Examination furniture has remarkable properties, which can tax the ingenuity and stamina of examination administrators. The first phenomenon comes to light when the preparations for the examination season get under way: it is at this point that it is generally discovered that a significant number of examination desks have been removed from stock and are in use in teaching rooms, or that the rooms from which examination desks are normally taken appear to have fewer desks than the inventory suggests should be the case. The solution for this is that the examinations administration must have the power within the institution to recover all examination desks from wherever in the institution they have migrated to, whether this is other teaching rooms, common rooms or (rather common) lecturing staff offices; where this is done, the examinations administration is under no obligation to provide replacements.

The second migrating desk phenomenon occurs overnight in examination rooms themselves. At the start of the examination the desks will have been put in neat ranks and files. The next morning most of the desks will have moved forward towards the front of the room, getting closer and closer to each other. This is caused by the human tendency, when seated behind a small desk, to leave the examination not by moving the chairs backwards (as one would do at, say, a dining table) but by pushing the desk forwards. The candidates for the next examination will sit down and tuck themselves up to the desk by drawing up their chair behind them. After a few examinations all the desks will be compressed into the space allocated for half as many rows. There is no practical solution to this other than to spend a few minutes each morning moving them all backwards and spreading them more evenly around the room.

There is a serious administrative implication behind the second feature described above. When allocating desk numbers to the room it is safest to do this column by column; doing it row by row results very quickly in the rows not being correctly aligned with each other, to the confusion of the students (and invigilators).

4.5   Special examination facilities

Not all students are able to take examinations in the way approved for that subject. Students may be affected by illness, accidents or personal circumstances. The number of cases appears to have grown rapidly over the past few decades: this may be a result of changes in the student profile (more mature students), but is more likely to be a reflection of the increasingly caring attitude of institutions.

There are two guiding factors in managing special examination facilities: fairness to the student and fairness to all the other students. It is of absolute importance that whatever special dispensations are made for a student with an illness, a disability or other extenuating circumstances are not perceived by other candidates to impart an actual advantage. If, for example, any extra time granted is too generous other students may feel disadvantaged by comparison. Such potential resentment arises more commonly if a student is permitted a different method of assessment: for example, if a student with a writing problem is permitted to do additional untimed essays rather than an invigilated examination, any students who feel that they themselves perform better in coursework than in examination could wish to complain. Colleagues of students with special facilities usually understand the need for these, but only if it redresses a disadvantage – not if it goes as far as to give a perceivedly unfair advantage.

Many special facilities can be provided relatively easily. Dyslexic students or those with writing problems can be given extra time (but not so much that it actually makes them too tired to perform well; an extra ten minutes per hour is a useful norm). In many cases, all the students with special facilities in a particular examination session can be accommodated together in an additional room (this is usually preferable to complicating the management of the main room). But not always – students who suffer from extreme agoraphobia or claustrophobia might have to be examined individually.

The main disadvantages in using individual examination rooms are that they increase the number of invigilators, and make it more difficult to communicate any corrections which may need to be made to the paper if discovered during the examination. If communal rooms are used for whole groups of students with special facilities they can best be supervised by one of the normal pool of invigilators; students with individual sessions should normally be invigilated by a member of staff from their department as part of the normal pastoral care provided by staff for their wards. In exceptional cases students may be permitted to take examinations at home, in hospital or in prison; even in these cases it is vital that the invigilation is provided by the institution (from the student's department) and not left to relatives, friends, doctors, nurses or other local staff. This is not to impute unreliability to such people, but to ensure that the examination is seen to be totally reputable.

Drawing up an institutional policy on special facilities is closely related to the drawing up of policy on mitigating circumstances. Very little relating to the human condition is constant: not all sprained wrists have the same effect on writing; not all relatives are so close that bereavement upsets the student's performance; not all dyslexia is equally severe. It is prudent to draw up guidelines so that the dispensations granted are roughly equivalent, but not to turn the guidelines into a simple tariff, since this introduces inequities. It can also be helpful if the decision on the special provisions to be allowed is determined centrally, to ensure parity of treatment.

As a matter of policy the institution should always require that the students submit acceptable evidence of whatever they claim necessitates the special facilities. For chronic conditions this will often not be necessary each year, but for accidents and unexpected personal disasters the institution must insist upon impartial corroboration.

If students with writing impairment are granted the use of computers, on the grounds that this is their normal method of composing, the institution should always supply the computer (it is often easiest to requisition a computer work area as an examination room) so that it can ensure that all the memory is clean. Only in really exceptional circumstances should students be permitted to use their own computer (for example, if it is specially adapted to cope with a disability): it is not that such students cannot be trusted not to have stored notes on the disks, but more (as noted above) that others can see that there is no opportunity for this to happen.

4.6 Marking

There is little to be said here about marking of examinations or coursework. Each institution must decide for itself any policy on double marking: does any second marker merely moderate the mark of the first marker, or is it completely re-marked without seeing the original marks, with the two marks reconciled mutually or by a third party? There are no particular administrative questions involved other than making sure that any policy is carried out.

What does have managerial implications is the policy on anonymous assessment. The need for anonymous marking is not a matter for administrative debate, and will therefore not be analysed here; only the administrative implications will be. Depending on the level of anonymity, the additional work involved in implementing anonymous assessment may fall differently on administrators and on markers. Anonymous assessment is not universal, or universally agreed to be worthwhile; nor is there a standard model.

The extent to which anonymity is preserved depends on where the bias occurs which the process is meant to avoid:

- *Written examinations*: the most common stage. Examination scripts bear numbers rather than names, the marks are allocated to the numbers and then allocated to the names ready for the mark sheets.
- *Essays*: less common. It is harder to preserve anonymity when essays are handed in or back by hand.
- *Decision stage*: this is even less common, though far from unknown. The board of examiners does not know the names of the candidates either, just anonymous mark sheets with a candidate number.
- *Mitigating evidence stage*: it is virtually impossible to preserve anonymity once the main marks have been agreed and mitigating evidence is being considered. Most attempts to do so are illusory, and it benefits no one to have sham anonymity at the expense of efficiency.
- *Results*: pass lists can be published anonymously with just candidate numbers if it saves delay between the board of examiners and the publication of the results, or if the institution has doubts about publishing named pass lists (see section 4.10). At this stage the issue is not about eliminating bias but preserving confidentiality.

Managing an anonymous assessment regime is not simply a matter of asking students to put a candidate number on their scripts rather than their name. There are significant extra loads placed on both academic and administrative staff:

- What number is used? Some feel that using the student's normal ID number undermines anonymity, since there could be several lists available which link numbers and names; however, issuing a separate number considerably increases the bureaucracy involved, not least in ensuring that the students receive notification of their number.
- Students are more likely to make mistakes with numbers than with their name. Giving them a candidate card with their number on it does not guarantee that they will remember to bring it with them. Giving invigilators a list on which they or the candidates can look up their number is cumbersome. Requiring invigilators to check that the numbers entered by each student agree with the lists of those expected is very burdensome. If an incorrect number is suspected or identified after the examination, how is the candidate's true number ascertained?
- There can be complications in associating anonymous examination scripts with marks from coursework; if the latter is not done anonymously the name of the candidate has to be ascertained before the marks can be added; if the coursework is marked anonymously there can be mistakes in identifying the correct association.

The main issue is correct collation of all of the marks, without introducing too many complications. It is not impossible to do accurately, but nor is it administratively simple to devise foolproof procedures.

4.7 Boards of examiners

The timing of boards of examiners has become more complex with the spread of modular courses. A very common practice on modular structures is to have two stages: a first round of meetings which consider the results of individual examinations in their subject group, and a second round of boards of examiners for the various courses on which these modules figure and which deals with the outcome of these first meetings. Where modules feed directly to a small range of courses this two-stage process is not really necessary, and if it can be avoided it certainly simplifies the administration and eases the load on the staff and the external examiners. All this complexity should have led to more time being provided for the processing of marksheets ready for the board of examiners, but such is the pressure on time that this has rarely been possible.

The effect of the added complexity of two-stage examiners boards is not just on the workload of the staff involved, and the extra attendance by external examiners; this very complexity itself has tended to put severe pressure on the schedule of meetings, with boards creeping further and further into what staff feel is the vacation period. To some extent that does not matter, since the demarcation between term-time and vacation has been continuously eroded over many years; the main negative impact of this is, however, that it is virtually impossible to guarantee giving students their results before they return home at the end of term.

The main load for the student administrator is naturally that of ensuring that all the paperwork for the meeting is complete: a complete set of marks, any mitigating evidence submitted by students or others, invitations to all those involved (ensuring quoracy), and, at the meeting, making sure that all students are considered and that their results are clear, complete and unambiguous. Where a final decision cannot be made at the meeting the secretary to the board must ensure that it is followed up speedily and approved by chair's action, with the agreement of any external examiners involved. The board should clearly state what process it has agreed for these deferred decisions: it may authorize the chair to take whatever action seems fit, it may set up a subgroup, it may decide to reconvene; all are legitimate ways of dealing with this.

4.8 Mitigating circumstances

The processing of submissions by students presenting evidence of mitigating circumstances for poor performance is very complex. It is also becoming more widespread, possibly because of the increased pressure on students to maximize their marks, as mentioned in section 4.11.

One of the first things to note is that there is no requirement on institutions to take any such evidence into account. If the institution wishes to make its decisions purely on the performance on the day of the assessment it is free to do so. However, it can only do so if it has not included any provision for mitigating circumstances in its procedures and regulations: if the board has powers to take such evidence into account, then it must do so if any is submitted.

One side-effect of the increase in submissions by students is possibly unfortunate: the number, variety and complexity of the cases tends to need a more formalized approach for dealing with them, yet having a form and advertised guidelines for submissions serves also to publicize the facility and to encourage yet more submissions. If fairness is one of the desiderata of the board this must be accepted as a better outcome than a system which discourages submissions. However, the board must avoid the natural compassion which could lead it to assume that all submissions are genuine and equally deserving of leading to a change in the outcome.

It is worth bearing in mind the points made in Chapter 8 (section 8.12) about judicial reviews. These have a strong bearing on the way in which mitigating evidence is processed, and they sometimes go against the natural instincts of those present. In particular it means that all relevant information must have been used insofar as this may be defined in the regulations; the board cannot take into account any extra information that is not permitted in regulations, nor should there be any vetting or simplification of the evidence by any person not authorized to do so in the regulations. For example, if the secretary were to sift the evidence before the meeting this could be challenged as unauthorized; if the chair were to do it, it might be acceptable; if the secretary analysed the submissions and tried to place them into 'strong' and 'weak' lists, that is also probably acceptable provided the basis for this categorization is also presented to the board, since the board is still the body which makes the decision itself. The secretary of the board of examiners is unlikely to be vested with powers of discretion over the outcome of board decisions.

Where the natural instincts of compassionate examiners run most strongly counter to the requirements of procedural propriety is where one or more of the members of the Board happens to know about circumstances which may have affected the performance of a student but the student himself or herself has not submitted this information as mitigating evidence. In almost all cases such evidence should *not* be taken into account. Only evidence explicitly submitted by the student should be considered; otherwise the board is acting on incomplete knowledge dependent on whoever happens to be on the board at the time. In some circumstances the student could take action against the board member for breach of confidence. Where this approach *is* probably acceptable is where the student is deemed by the board to be in no state to make a reasonable submission: for example, being unconscious or otherwise incapacitated. Notwithstanding this, as it should be taking into account the student's perception of the effect on their performance rather than just the medical facts, the board should really defer a decision on such a student until his or her views can be heard.

As will be seen from the discussion on judicial reviews in Chapter 8 (section 8.12), the consideration of mitigating circumstances in no way guarantees to the student that the mark actually achieved will be changed. The board has to judge whether the student's performance is below expectations because of the circumstances: it cannot simply raise a mark because of illness if that mark appears to reflect accurately the student's ability. For this reason, if it comes to a judicial review, the courts will only need to see that the evidence was considered: they do not need to see the debate or the outcome. A corollary of this is that the secretary should try not to record more than is strictly needed in the minutes of the meeting for such students; going into too much detail can lead to claims that the wording chosen betrays a prejudiced or dismissive approach. The less there is recorded, the less there is to be challenged, but the fact that evidence was considered must itself be minuted.

Practices differ as to when mitigating circumstances should be considered. If there is a single-stage board of examiners it can obviously be done at that stage; however, it is not so clear where consideration should take place when the institution has a two-stage board of examiners.

- Considering mitigating circumstances at the first stage, the subject stage, ensures that the view of whether there has been an effect on performance is being given by those best placed to understand that particular examination. However, where a condition has covered several examinations different views may be held by the individual examiners boards. This is not in itself proof of inconsistency: a broken finger, for example, may affect performance on a written examination but not on a practical one; dyslexia may affect an essay but not affect a mathematical test.

- Considering mitigating circumstances at the second stage, the course stage, ensures comparability of treatment across all the modules taken by that student, but loses the subject context.
- It is vital that consideration is not given independently at both stages, as that will lead to double compensation in many cases.
- A compromise adopted in many institutions is for the first-stage board to recommend to the second-stage board that evidence considered is sufficient for marks to be adjusted if the student is otherwise on a borderline between pass and fail, or for a higher classification. If such an approach is used it must be clear whether the first-stage committee is recommending a particular outcome, or just marking that record as being worthy of reconsideration if necessary. This sounds a fair compromise but it may create rather cumbersome procedures, and it can mean that only those students who are on borderlines have their marks adjusted for mitigating circumstances.

Irrespective of which committee considers the mitigating evidence it is preferable to consider all cases at once, i.e. at the *end* of the meeting rather than as they come up in the overall list of students; this helps to ensure overall comparability, since each decision can be made in the context of the overall range of cases submitted. Those who attend many boards of examiners will be familiar with comments from members to the effect that 'if I'd known this case was coming up I'd have argued differently on the earlier one', or 'I could have said the same for X if I'd known the board would have considered it at all relevant.' The regrettable feature of comments of this sort is that they imply that the speaker believes that the evidence really is not relevant, but that parity must be observed; parity and equity are laudable aims, but not at the expense of common sense.

Given the rise in the number of cases for the reasons mentioned above, it is increasingly common for the boards of examiners to delegate detailed consideration of the cases to a subcommittee. This is not contrary to the points made above about the sovereignty of the board of examiners, provided that if the subcommittee meets before the board it does not make the final decision but passes recommendations to the board; it cannot do otherwise, since the academic consideration of the marks achieved will not yet have taken place. Alternatively, the board of examiners can identify cases which have mitigating evidence submitted, agree what the academic outcome would be if there were no acceptable evidence and then empower the subcommittee to decide if the decision should be modified; any changes must be approved by the chair and any external examiner appointed for that course. It does not really matter whether such a subcommittee covers just one course, or a group of related courses, or all the courses for that faculty or department; a committee for the whole institution would probably find itself swamped.

4.9   Aegrotat and posthumous awards

The position of aegrotat and posthumous awards is discussed in greater detail in Chapter 5 (section 5.8).

4.10   Release of marks

When all the examination processes are complete, the students must be told their results. Almost all institutions now give students precise marks or grades for each module or area of assessment, though this is a relatively modern phenomenon. The increase in the role of coursework introduced a new concept of the 'provisional mark', the role of which must be clearly explained to students: any mark released to the student before the meeting of the board of examiners may be changed by that board without the need to give an explanation (usually it is merely that the marks have been moderated or scaled, not that a particular student's mark still needs adjustment by the final stages).

The chair of the board and the external examiner must agree to any procedures involving release of provisional marks, since they are the people who will have to deal with any objections from students who have not grasped that 'provisional' means more than simply 'waiting to be confirmed'. The provisions of the institution's registration under data protection legislation should also be checked (see Chapter 9) in case the method of releasing marks in a public way (e.g. pinning mark lists to notice boards) should be felt by students who have failed to be publicly humiliating for them.

4.11   Examination reviews and appeals

An 'examination review' is normally defined as a request to have an assessment re-marked. An 'appeal' is against a perceived injustice in the procedure, whether as a result of a mistake or of deliberate action. The further category of 'complaint' is not covered here, as it covers behaviour and treatment rather than procedures, and has no particularly distinct features when it involves students as opposed to any other person.

Reviews of examination marks used to be rare: many institutions did not even have procedures whereby a student could challenge the mark awarded. Appeals have a longer history, although it is still largely the case that a student lodging an appeal cannot do so as a challenge to the academic judgement of the examiners, but only on the grounds that a piece of work (essay, examination script) has been lost or otherwise unfairly disregarded, or that the coursework marks awarded were different from those fed back to the student during the year. In effect there is a challenge to the process of marking, not to the judgement behind the marks.

As the temptations of litigation increase, and as the increasing participation rate in higher education has increased the perceived stigma of not having a degree, there is possibly more at stake now for the student who is awarded a low mark or a fail grade: this means that many students who are disappointed with their results feel that there is nothing to lose by requesting a review of the mark, or by appealing against the process. There is an unfortunate tendency among academic staff, especially those more used to the less litigious days of the relatively recent past, to assume that a student would not ask for a review unless something had indeed gone wrong, with the resultant reluctance to turn down requests for reviews: this merely encourages all students to challenge any mark, even if they know in their hearts that the mark is a true reflection of their ability. This attitude appears to have gone hand in hand with the less deferential attitude to higher education in general, and the lecturing staff in particular (as, indeed, has happened to education at all levels). Where the impartiality of the markers is called into question, it is very useful if more than one person has been involved, either as a 'second marker' or as an external examiner moderating all the marks. On the other hand, the rise in the number of appeals is possibly also a side-effect of the laudable increase in policies of releasing marks to students: now that they can see how close they are to a higher classification, there is more to be gained if just one extra mark can move them over a borderline.

It must not be assumed that all student appeals are aimed at securing a higher mark or a better outcome. There have been cases of students appealing against a pass mark because they wanted to be required to stay a further year before returning home. In other cases students have wished appeal against a pass mark as a fail mark would be part of a claim against an institution for poor supervision (with a view to a refund of fees), or have wished to prove to separated parents that their divorce has ruined their degree, only to find their cases undermined by excellent examination results. An appeal against over-generous marking for self-confessed poor performance can be very embarrassing.

4.12 Examination review and appeal procedures

In Chapter 8 (section 8.12), on legal aspects of student administration, there is a discussion of the role of judicial reviews in the statutory institutions. Similarly, student complaints and appeals in the chartered institutions are routed to the 'visitor', who has exclusive jurisdiction in relation to the contract between the student and the higher education institution; particular care must be taken in partnerships between two institutions where one uses the visitor system and the other does not. One of the main areas where an institution may find itself under a judicial review is in appeals against results and classifications. Any student who feels that the rules have not been followed (other than in a very mechanistic way such as faulty arithmetic) may feel it worth challenging them before a judge. In such cases the judge will not only subject the regulations to intense scrutiny but also (and indeed primarily) consider carefully whether they have been followed. Meticulous care must be taken to ensure that procedures are followed to the letter: exceeding them (even if trying to be helpful) can be as damaging in a court hearing as not meeting them. Discretion must only have been used where the regulations permit it, and if it is permitted it *must* be considered. Local tradition and unwritten conventions overriding the written regulations will normally be rejected by the judge as unauthorized.

Appeals can arise particularly commonly with submissions of mitigating evidence for poor performance; this is covered in greater detail in section 4.8 above.

Cases subjected to judicial appeal still seem to confirm that the courts will not consider a challenge to the academic judgement of the board of examiners or the examiners themselves. The challenge of 'unreasonable' outcomes mentioned in Chapter 8 (section 8.8) is possibly only of relevance to procedures and decisions, not to judgements and marks; even if referred back by judicial review, the court cannot make the examiners change the mark when revisited. Thus, the remote chance of student success at judicial review can be a hollow victory, since the examiners need only revisit the marking process, carefully following the exact procedures prescribed in the regulations, and may well come up with the same academic result the second time around.

4.13 Cheating ▰

The incidence of cheating is growing; or perhaps institutions are getting better at catching it. There appears to be little doubt that the pressure on students to succeed is greater than ever.

One of the ironies of this is that it may be a function of the fact that a higher proportion of people are going on to further and higher education. When only a small percentage of privileged scholars had degrees, there was no stigma in not having one, and many extremely intelligent people did not have degrees. Now that a very high proportion have further or higher education qualifications of some sort, the effect of not having one can be serious both financially and psychologically.

Making this an even more complicated pressure is the fact that merely having a qualification no longer guarantees a brilliant job or funding for research afterwards; there is therefore a heightened desire (often even a desperation) not just to pass but to pass with a very good classification. Professional bodies increase this pressure by erecting an inflexible hurdle for membership: for example, an honours degree at 'upper second' level. The pressure to get that extra few marks can be intense, leading to cheating and persistent appeals by students who really know what their true performance is, and who in other circumstances would not dream of fraud. Family pressure can be quite explicit and burdensome on students, though very often this is more hidden as the student feels a moral duty to repay parental investment by performing well. As students pay quite heavily from their own pockets too (fees, debts, etc.) they also want to get something for their own investment, at all costs and at whatever risk.

One form of cheating that students have to learn to avoid is 'plagiarism'. Very many students start further or higher education from a background where good marks for work could be obtained by repeating what they had been taught in class or read in books; marks for independent thinking may not be common in such environments. Suddenly students find themselves not only getting low marks for mere repetition of passages from hand-outs and books, but also possibly being charged with cheating for doing so. This also appears to be a difficult concept if students have been educated in a culture where direct repetition of an expert's words is seen as *good* scholarship and demonstration of knowledge; in these circumstances students can be genuinely perplexed, and severely distressed at being accused of cheating. Good, clear guidelines must be issued to students, particularly in their first year, and first offences should be treated leniently if the examiner is sure that the plagiarism is naive or innocent.

That is not to say that all plagiarism is inadvertent. The existence of essay banks is hardly new, but the easy availability of essays (even PhD dissertations) complete and ready written on electronic sources has increased the temptation. Technology has also made detection more difficult in another way: word-processed essays make it harder to spot inserted or impersonated work than hand-written work. It is unfortunately not always easy to prove plagiarism unless a particular wording is prominent (although some students are unwise enough to leave passages in their work which make it easy to see that it is taken from elsewhere, sometimes even the name of the author or the other student involved, non-existent cross-references, etc.). Merely feeling that the work is too good to be the unaided effort of the student is unlikely to be a good defence if the student challenges a cheating penalty in a court of law. It is prudent to include a statement on a cover sheet for any submitted coursework whereby students confirm that they understand what plagiarism is, and that submitted work is entirely their own; this has the double benefit of increasing aware-ness of plagiarism and of making prosecution of cheating more straightforward by removing the possibility of claiming ignorance. Such cover sheets, if properly receipted, also have the benefit of prov-ing that a piece of work was submitted (false submission claims are quite a common means of attempted cheating).

A fairly rare problem is that of impersonation in examinations; or at least it is assumed to be rare. As student populations get larger, and their examinations get correspondingly larger, and the tutors become less able to recognize their charges, there is increased risk of students employing others to sit their examinations for them. If possible stud-ents should show their ID cards upon entry to the examination room, or display them on their desks. Any suspected impersonation must be treated as a very severe breach of regulations, with the maximum penalty. If the impersonator is another student from that institution, both of them should be dealt with under the disciplinary regulations. In this connection it is vital that the institution's cheating regulations are phrased to cover not only 'attempting to gain an unfair advantage' but also 'assisting others to gain an unfair advantage'; otherwise the impersonator might not be able to be charged, which would be most undesirable.

Impersonation in coursework is harder to catch, since the imper-sonator is not seen by the examiner. Students are often encouraged to work together as part of a valid learning experience. It is a tempt-ingly short step from that to pooling the coursework. The former is valid and laudable, the latter is cheating.

The most important way of managing cheating in examinations or coursework is to make sure that students understand:

- what it is;
- what happens to them if they do it;
- how to avoid doing it accidentally;
- that penalties will be imposed rigorously and fairly.

The responsibility for ensuring that students know this is shared between the tutors (who can give specific examples of pitfalls relating to their subject) and managers (who must make sure the regulations are known, implemented and carried out promptly and fairly).

Care must also be taken to ensure that all cheating definitions, procedures and penalties are consistent with those of any related professional bodies. For example, at least one professional body defines cheating with respect to written examinations only, and does not mention plagiarism: a student could therefore be guilty of internal breach for plagiarism but innocent under the professional body's rules. However, if a professional body's penalties are felt severe by the subject specialists concerned within the institution, a circumspect line must be negotiated between avoiding excessive side-effects for relatively minor offences and being perceived as being generous to these students merely because they have a professional body involvement. Fairness and equity to all students is paramount.

4.14   Access to old papers

A popular hobby among students is 'question spotting': collating questions from old papers to try to spot which ones come up most frequently, and whether any come round on regular cycles. This is good fun, and can have good educational value if it identifies key issues, but can be very misleading as a revision tool. If students are encouraged to look too far back in old papers they may be severely misled by subsequent changes in the syllabus making earlier questions irrelevant. Students should not normally be given access to previous issues of multiple-choice papers which draw on a fixed 'question bank'.

Underlying an institution's policy on access to old papers is its philosophy on examining: should examiners test what is taught (i.e. there should be questions on every topic taught, and on nothing else), or sample what is learned (i.e. there need not be a question on every topic taught, and the questions can cover anything in the subject even if not taught in class). Which of these is best is a pedagogic question outside the scope of this book, but the implications noted above must not be ignored.

4.15 Examinations in other countries ▐

As mentioned in section 4.2 and in Chapter 8 (section 8.6(d)), institutions sometimes deem it appropriate to permit students from other countries to take their examinations in their own country. The management of this raises special questions, and puts more responsibility not only on the administrative staff but also on the examiner. Similar considerations apply to ancillary centres (e.g. partner colleges) in the home country, but the problems are reduced by the proximity of the home institution.

Sending examination materials to another country can be slow and expensive. The institution must be sure that the question papers are sent securely and delivered to a person with appropriate authority, and must also send answer books and any supplementary documents such as data tables. Faxing a question paper may be tolerated in an emergency but is not suitable (and is very expensive) for data books, case studies, etc.

Despite the most careful preparations, examination papers and completed scripts do get lost when travelling internationally. No matter what assurances couriers may give, the package remains just one of many for them, and in the absence of the addressee they are very prone simply to hand it over to anyone they can find. Many examination packages have totally disappeared in this way. If the institution is absolutely sure that a question paper is mislaid beyond recovery it may decide to take the risk of sending a further copy; it remains a risk, however, as confidentiality may have been compromised. If there is any suspicion that a paper has been deliberately 'opened by mistake', or the contents made public in any other way, the institution must retain the right to declare that examination void for all candidates, not just for those at the examination place involved. A replacement paper must be set, the request for which is not always well received by the examiner.

Lost answer scripts are irreplaceable: it is prudent to arrange for fax copies to be sent first, followed by the paper originals separately.

The main impact on the examiner, if candidates are sitting examinations in another centre, is that the examinations office will probably be setting an earlier deadline for the completion of the question paper. This is more of an issue for examinations held at relatively short notice (e.g. resit examinations): to allow adequate time for posting the examination materials may substantially reduce the lead time available for the examiner.

Great care should be taken to select a centre in the other country which is acceptable in terms of facilities, supervision and reliability. If no obviously suitable centre is available the institution must retain the right to refuse permission for the examination to be taken in the student's home country. The most commonly acceptable locations are other higher education institutions, and offices of an embassy or national cultural centre (such as the British Council). It is not usually acceptable to arrange for examinations to be taken at schools, where the examination procedures may be very different, or with the student's employers unless it is a large multinational firm with a well established education and training centre; supervision in the normal place of work should never be acceptable.

4.16 External examiners

External examiners have a long and honoured role in higher education in the United Kingdom. They were originally appointed when colleges were offering external degrees from the University of London: the university sent one of its representatives to ensure that the standard of these degrees was comparable to that of those awarded within the university itself. When more institutions were empowered to confer their own degrees they took over this idea of external peer review. Since then the role of the external examiners has developed to encompass not only guarantees of parity of standard, but also a role as arbiter on awkward cases. The rapid increase in student numbers in the later years of the twentieth century, and the increasing complexity of courses, has led to several reviews of this role, and the future role may well differ from that described above.

The main concern of the student administrator in connection with external examiners is to ensure that the terms of their appointment, their powers and their responsibilities are very clearly and fully explained (including, crucially, whether they have the right to overrule a decision of the board, rather than merely having an extremely influential voice), and to ensure that any reports which they are required to submit are reasonably prompt and comprehensive. External examiners' reports are increasingly being scrutinized as part of an institution's quality assurance procedures, and the reporting and feedback mechanisms must not be inadequate. Questions of policy on the role of the external examiners, whether directed by internal needs or government policies, are beyond the scope of this book (see Piper 1994).

4.17 Mistakes and corrections

Mistakes are regrettable; mistakes are also inevitable. Students under examination pressure make mistakes. Examiners and boards of examiners make mistakes. The most important thing to do is minimize them, and know how to correct them when they are discovered.

If a mistake is discovered in a question paper, the correction must be conveyed to all ancillary centres where there are candidates (partner colleges, students being invigilated separately with special facilities, etc). Corrections should be determined only by the examiner or, if not available, a subject specialist: invigilators and administrators must resist the temptation to use common sense to correct apparent mistakes, since that might leave the candidates feeling on future occasions that they can negotiate a better interpretation of the question by persuading the invigilator that the present wording does not make sense. If a correction cannot be determined the invigilator must advise the students to use their own interpretation, and must submit a report on the unresolved problem which the marker must take into account.

Boards of examiners are responsible for their decisions. Changes to their decisions must therefore also be authorized by them. If others could freely change the decisions of boards of examiners there would be little point in having them. It follows from this that if a decision of a board of examiners needs to be changed, the board must authorise the change; this applies whether it is the correction of a mistake, or a change arising from an appeal of the discovery of any other information which renders the original decision invalid.

Since boards of examiners meet infrequently, the normal mechanism for changing decisions is for the chair of the board to act on its behalf; all such changes must be reported back to the next meeting of the board, so that it can monitor whether there has been excessive use of chair's action, and, if so, whether this is because of serious flaws in the processes or some other cause which needs remedying for the future. In the particular case of boards of examiners it is wise (and should be mandatory) for all changes to be agreed with any external examiner; at the very least this exonerates the chair from most accusations of carrying out a cover-up.

However the correction is made, it is important that all those to whom the original decision was given should be informed of the change, if it affects the processing of the record. This may not be necessary if it is a minor change of mark, but can be very important if it changes a student's status or progression.

An interesting (and sometimes contentious) procedural point about changing marks arises when an external examiner receives a sample of work rather than the whole batch, and feels that some or all of the pieces of work should have a higher or lower mark. A change of marks based on this alone is most inadvisable if it is done only for the students chosen as a random set for the external: if there are questions about the standards of marking, all the candidates on that module must be checked again, as otherwise students who by chance were disadvantaged by not being included in that sample may win an appeal.

Above all, the student must be informed, even if the change is not the result of an appeal or other action instigated by the student. The primary rule, in these cases as in most others, is not to attempt to conceal the mistake, as this almost inevitably results in a chain of ever deeper holes out of which the institution must dig itself, and which will attract very serious public criticism if there is a judicial review or complaints by the student.

(*Comment from the Series Editors*. See Chapter 8 concerning the legal aspects of student management, especially, as has been stressed in this chapter, in relation to the careful and consistent application of the institution's regulations *in every case*, never varying the regulations to suit the circumstances: following the regulations, adhering to the rules of natural justice ('due process' in US legal terms) and complying with procedural propriety is the best protection against the threat of judicial review in the statutory institutions and reference to the 'visitor' in the chartered institutions. See also the relevant chapters in Palfreyman and Warner (1998) concerning the student–HEI contract, student complaints and appeals, judicial review, the role of the visitor and the litigation process – together with similar coverage in Farrington (1998). It needs always to be noted, with some degree of comfort, that the courts, as stated above, while interested in whether procedures have been properly applied, will *not* attempt to peer through the veil of expert academic judgement, will *not* attempt to second-guess whether the physics examination script was a 2i or a 2ii, whether the theology thesis was pass or fail – and this is the case even in the USA, the land of litigation.)

5

AWARDS CEREMONIES
AND CERTIFICATES

The various sorts of ceremonies there are, why we have
them, who should go, and who officiates.

Thrice-gorgeous ceremony.

(William Shakespeare, *Henry V*, IV.i.286)

Prepare not to be gone; we have a trifling foolish banquet.

(William Shakespeare, *Romeo and Juliet*, I.v.125)

5.1 Why have awards ceremonies? What is 'graduation'?

Awards ceremonies in the United Kingdom have their origins in the
granting of a licence to teach, conferred by the bishop of a diocese,
and having effect only within that diocese. In the middle ages the
authority to confer degrees on students was vested only in the institution's chancellor or vice-chancellor, under powers delegated from
the church. However, only the Pope could give authority to teach
in more than one diocese; this meant that when King Henry VIII
assumed the powers previously exercised by the Pope, during the
Reformation, this power was transferred to the Crown. This also
explains why older universities could only be created by a royal
charter. In later times, the awards ceremony became more secular,
and had no necessary link with a licence to teach.

The idea of a student rising through the various stages from novice
to master is reflected in the terminology: the first stage degree con-
tinued to be called a 'bachelor' (see below), meaning 'novice' who
'graduates' by taking a step (Latin *gradus*, step) on the way to becoming a 'master'.

Higher education has still to find terms which are not gender-
specific for these awards, though it should be noted that the origin

of the word 'bachelor' probably did not relate especially to males: its origin is not entirely clear, but one proposed derivation is from 'cowherd' (vulgar Latin vacca, a cow), via the intermediate meanings of 'farm hand', 'general assistant', 'trainee' and 'novice'. Once the students have completed the final step, they are 'graduates', i.e. 'those who have stepped'.

Some institutions use the term 'graduand' (i.e. 'one who is stepping') to cover the student's status between successfully completing the course and having the award formally conferred: the change from 'graduand' to 'graduate' takes place at the moment at which the person officiating utters the words 'I admit you to the degree', or the person officiating completes whatever ceremonial is involved (bow, handshake, etc.).

It can be seen from the above that the terms 'graduate' and 'graduand' should, on semantic grounds, be used only for students receiving a degree. There is no easy phrase to cover those receiving certificates and diplomas; the latter may be referred to as 'diplomates', though this can cause confusion with 'diplomats', and is felt to be artificial by some, especially as it is impossible to construct a similar word for those receiving 'certificates'. In general no great harm is done, except perhaps to those who view etymology and derivation as the sole criterion for word usage, if the terms 'graduands' and 'graduates' are applied to all those receiving an award.

For awards other than degrees no licence was needed, so certificates and diplomas could be conferred by any body which took upon itself the power to do so. Many of these evolved into, or generated, the professional and statutory bodies which regulate the conferral of many awards which carry with them a licence to practise, or educational bodies which attempt to confer an equality of standards by validating courses at a wide variety of institutions towards a common award.

5.2   What is the function of the ceremony?

There are two basic types of ceremony: the conferral ceremony and the celebration ceremony. The difference may appear relatively trivial but it fundamentally controls what happens at the ceremonies, and who can act at them.

(a) The 'conferral' ceremony

A ceremony which is the actual mechanism for conferring the award presupposes that the results have come from a board of examiners as recommendations to the officially empowered committee of the institution, such as the senate, the academic board or the board of governors, and that the latter ratifies the recommendation and puts them forward for conferral. If a ceremony's role is to enact the formal conferral of the award, the following implications must be borne in mind.

A student may have been recommended for an award by a board of examiners, but is not a 'graduate' until the ceremony has taken place. Until that time the student is merely *eligible* to receive the award but has not yet done so. The act of conferral is what legally brings into existence the award for that student.

It follows from this that no certificates can be issued in advance of the ceremony, since the award has not yet been conferred. It is certainly permissible to issue transcripts, but if issued before the conferral ceremony they ought not to say 'has received the degree of X', but rather 'is eligible to receive the degree of X, which is due to be conferred on date Y'. It is best, when drafting such wording, not to guarantee that the award will be conferred, for the reasons outlined below (e.g. late debts). Such wordings are probably easier to devise for 'to whom it may concern' letters than on official transcripts. In most cases little harm will be done if a transcript implies that the award has been conferred, provided that it is clear that it is only a transcript and not a certificate itself. The effect on the issue of certificates can sometimes be difficult to explain to students: if they are not actually attending the ceremony they may not understand why their certificate cannot be issued to them in advance instead of having to wait until after the ceremony.

It also follows that, not being a graduate, the student cannot yet add the award letters (BA, etc.) after their name. Although technically true, it is doubtful if any institution would take action against any of its former students who did so unless it was done to gain fraudulent access to rights to which the student was not yet entitled, or to imply that the conferral had taken place when it had actually been suspended. It would also be a strange employer who refused to engage a graduate purely on the technicality that the ceremony had not been held yet.

Similarly, the student is technically not allowed to wear the academic dress which belongs to the award. Some institutions are more concerned about this than others.

One effect of making the ceremony the act which formally confers the award is that a student whose award misses the ceremony will probably have to wait until the next ceremony in order to become a graduate: this may be one year into the future. This will affect those students who are very late in settling their accounts or other obligations (such as library books), those whose results were delayed because of late completion of work (perhaps due to illness) and those whose course does not run in the same academic year as the other courses.

The level of sympathy which an institution will have for these cases will vary according to the cause. If the delay is caused by the action or inaction of the student (e.g. debt clearance) it may be felt that the likelihood of a one-year delay in conferral is part of the mechanism for encouraging prompt payment; if the delay is caused by illness there may be greater sympathy in finding alternative solutions, such as a conferral by chair's action; if the delay is caused by structural aspects of the course delivery the institution may decide to hold a separate ceremony just for the students on the course concerned. Even that solution has its complexities: if an institution is having a small ceremony in the middle of the year for a specific set of courses, will it also allow stragglers from the main ceremonies to have their awards conferred at the ceremony, or will it regard the ceremony as exclusively for the course intended? A decision either way can offend some of those involved.

Defining the ceremony as the 'conferral event' can make minor ceremonies, such as those described in the previous paragraph, a little more complex than their scope or size might suggest: they still need to be held with the same structure and powers as a 'full' ceremony. This is particularly awkward if there is a separate ceremony for partner colleges or a ceremony held elsewhere in the world for the institution's graduates from another country. The principal, chancellor, vice-chancellor or other approved person (see below) will need to be present at each one: it cannot simply be left to a local proxy.

In a way the converse of the above position is that in which the institution may find itself if, because of a mistake made by the institution, the graduate could not attend the conferral ceremony, and whose award is therefore made 'in absentia' (see section 5.13). If the student asks for the right to attend a later ceremony the institution has a dilemma: to agree may constitute double conferral, but to refuse could create a very poor public relations approach. Most institutions find a way of permitting students to attend a later ceremony, and annotate their records to show that it was a deferred attendance, as this could otherwise lead to the later date showing on the certificate as the 'date of conferral'. As with so many other aspects of student administration, the best interests of the student take precedence over the formality of regulations.

A ceremony which is constituted as a conferral event requires the presence of someone authorized to confer awards in the institution's statutes or regulations. In the case of higher education institutions, this will almost certainly be primarily the chancellor, principal or chair of the board of governors; the vice-chancellor will also almost certainly have these powers defined in his or her role. If it is the chancellor's, principal's or vice-chancellor's custom or need to empower others (such as pro-vice-chancellors) to confer awards, this power must be declared in the statutes or regulations, preferably with an indication of the normal scope of that power. For example, does the vice-chancellor have total discretion as to who receives this delegated power, or must it be a senior academic? Can it include the academic registrar? There are no legal constraints on this, other than that whoever delegates must have the power of delegation in this matter (see Chapter 8, section 8.14). For example, if the institution's statutes vest the power only in the chancellor, the chancellor may not arrogate to himself or herself the power to delegate further to others the authority to officiate at a ceremony.

If the institution has decided that its ceremony is the means by which awards are conferred, it would also be prudent to define a mechanism whereby an individual award can be conferred without a formal ceremony. This is relatively easy to arrange if the institution's statutes merely define the persons with the power to confer and do not prescribe a mechanism or the need for a formally convened assembly: some regulations require that 'the university' is present, or at least imply this by saying that the awards are conferred 'in the presence of the university' or some such wording. Subject to any constraints of that nature, it is usually possible to arrange that an award can be conferred as an individual act by the person authorized, so that the vice-chancellor or principal can confer the award by a sort of 'chair's action' on behalf of the ceremony. This is an exceedingly useful facility, but should not be overused; normally it will only need to be used where a student has accidentally been omitted from a ceremony, or where there are other reasons for not insisting that the student wait until the next formal ceremony. However, it would be wrong to see this as a defensive mechanism, only of use to cover up mistakes or to avoid disputes with contentious debtors. The power to confer awards by executive action has, in the past, been a very positive way of being able to confer an award upon a terminally ill student without the rigmarole of convening a minimal 'ceremony'.

To facilitate actions such as those described in the previous paragraph, an institution should avoid defining a minimum quorum for its ceremonies, other than a person authorized to confer awards. If the statutes declare that the ceremony is an 'assembly' or 'congregation' of the university, legal advice may be sought on what this term means as regards a quorum: it probably means very little other than that the ceremony is properly held by an authorized person.

(b) The 'celebration' ceremony

In institutions where the boards of examiners themselves formally confer the award as part of their decision, subject usually to confirmation and ratification by the vice-chancellor, the senate, the academic board or the board of governors, the awards ceremony itself does not have the legal function described in the previous paragraph for 'conferral ceremonies'. To some this may devalue the role of the ceremony, but to others it may make it more relaxed and enjoyable.

For a ceremony which is purely celebratory without a formal conferral function, the points made in the preceding section are reversed: the student is a 'graduate' as soon as the authorized committee has approved the decision; certificates can be issued straight away; the graduate can immediately add the award letters after his or her name and wear academic dress; a student who misses the ceremony is still a graduate; minor 'catching up' ceremonies are not needed, etc.

In terms purely of the administration of the ceremony, the differences manifest themselves in not having to ensure the presence of an authorized person to confer the awards, and being able to permit students to attend twice, or attend the 'wrong' ceremony, without causing constitutional tangles.

Celebratory ceremonies have a very real role to play even in those institutions which have a formal conferral ceremony. This arises when the institution wishes to permit separate ceremonies at partner colleges, or ceremonies in other countries for the graduates from that country who have studied at the institution that year. To avoid the complications of having separate conferral ceremonies it is often easier to present the names of these students to the conferral ceremony, but to arrange a local celebration for the college or country concerned. For partner colleges this can often be done as part of their own end-of-year celebrations, at which, for example, they may also be conferring awards of their own. In this case all that is desirable is that someone is present from the parent institution: it does not need to be one of those authorized to confer awards, but can, for example, be a dean or even the academic registrar or head of public relations; for events in other countries the person charged with the welfare of foreign students (dean of international students, international officer, etc.) may be the most appropriate.

If a local partner celebration is being held as an adjunct to a main conferral ceremony, there is a slight risk of the celebration being presented by enthusiastic local administrators (often with understandable local pride) as if it is a conferral ceremony. This need not be a major problem unless the representatives of the guest institution are made to feel that they are there almost as an irrelevance or a mere token presence, and that the conferral at their institution was a mere formality before the 'real' event. There is also a slight risk if the local event is held before the conferral ceremony, because, for the reasons given above, the students may not yet technically be graduates and therefore not entitled to wear academic dress or receive their certificates; the inability to do this can be felt to detract strongly from the local ceremony. There are two solutions to this: the vice-chancellor can formally confer the awards by chair's action (see section 5.2(a) above) before the local ceremony, so that they are graduates; or the institution can make sure that all local ceremonies are held *after* the conferral ceremony.

Ceremonies which are celebratory, rather than having a conferral function, also tend to fit more comfortably with any tradition of issuing prizes, cups or other non-award accolades. In institutions whose main ceremony has conferral powers these ancillary awards tend to be issued at local departmental events, not only as a means of preserving departmental pride but also to reduce the length and complexity of the conferral ceremony.

Celebratory ceremonies do not really need to consider the question of awards *in absentia*. They may, nevertheless, wish to make tribute to the achievements of those not present.

There is no legal constraint on whether an institution chooses to have a conferral ceremony or a celebratory ceremony. Each institution can choose its own model, but must ensure that its statutes and regulations are consistent with the decided practices and procedures. Many institutions find that having a conferral ceremony imparts a greater sense of dignity to the proceedings, though others would see this as unnecessary pomp.

5.3 The position with partner colleges

Various points have been raised with respect to arrangements for partner colleges. There is a slight difference which is often respected between, on the one hand, partnerships where a college runs, under a franchise arrangement, a course belonging to the other institution, and, on the other hand, a relationship where one institution validates the awards of the other institution. Normally one would expect awards made as validations to be conferred as a separate ceremony at the institution running the course; franchise relationships tend to be more evenly split between local 'conferral' ceremonies and local 'celebratory' ceremonies run after the main conferral ceremony at the parent institution.

5.4 Interim awards

Most conferral ceremonies do not issue 'interim' awards, largely on the grounds that the ceremonies are already complex and long enough without them. The awards concerned are those to which a student achieves an eligibility while continuing on their main course. This has become more of an issue with the rise of modular courses and credit accumulation structures. It is very common to describe multiple exit points on courses, such as CertHE after a certain number of credits, a DipHE after some more credits, a degree without honours for a larger number of credits and a degree with honours for the normal maximum number of credits. Although a student working through the course will inevitably have enough credits for one or other of these interim awards at the end of each year of study, it is not normal for the awards to be formally awarded or conferred. To do so would require either that a student who completed the course ended up with multiple awards (BA, DipHE, CertHE . . .), or that each higher award cancelled out or upgraded the earlier one. The complexity of this is not recommended.

One exception to this might be where the interim award is the professional stage qualification, and therefore needs to be explicitly conferred. Some professional bodies, for example, use the postgraduate diploma as the professional qualification, with the upgrade to MA/MSc as an optional extra: in these cases the institution may decide that it confers both qualifications. If the ceremony is purely celebratory this question does not arise, and the decision as to whether these students can attend is really just a matter of whether the ceremony will be too large if they are there. In extreme cases it could involve every student attending for an award every year – if that is what the institution wants, there is no reason why they should not do so.

5.5 Issue of certificates

The handover of certificates is not governed by whether the ceremony is for conferral or for celebration, subject to the single constraint mentioned in section 5.2(a), i.e. that certificates cannot be issued before the award has been conferred. There is no requirement to issue certificates at a ceremony, whatever its status: the advantage of doing so in making it a better ceremony has to be offset against the administrative complexity and tension involved in ensuring that each student receives the correct certificate in the very tightly constrained circumstances of the ceremony.

5.6 The range in style of awards ceremonies

The range in style of ceremonies is wide.

(a) *'Oxbridge'*. At one extreme of the spectrum of ceremonial styles lies the very traditional 'Oxbridge' ceremony. This may be conducted largely or entirely in Latin (leading to some intriguing neologisms for course titles), and have very formalized ritual approaches to the presentation of the graduands to the vice-chancellor to receive their degrees (including the Oxford 'proctors' walk' where the two proctors walk up and down the Sheldonian Theatre 'inviting' tugs at their gowns if anyone objects to a particular individual receiving his or her degree, or the Cambridge custom of presenting students to the vice-chancellor four at a time, each holding one of the praelector's fingers in his or her right hand).

(b) *Formal*. Most non-Oxbridge institutions adopt a less formal approach than the ancient universities; at least in not using Latin. This does not necessarily mean that the ceremonies are informal; far from it. A great deal of pomp and ritual is still present in the ceremonies: some of them involve local traditions based on various historical activities whose purpose has long since become obscure. The structure of the ceremonies is typically formal, with set pieces for a keynote speech from the chancellor or principal, presentation of honorary awards, academic processions, etc.

(c) *Informal*. At the other extreme from the Oxbridge model is the ceremony which is simply a celebration of student achievement. There need be very little ceremony, and even less ritual.

Which model to use? There is, as is so often the case, no right or wrong answer. A 'formal' ceremony does not need to be sombre, nor does an 'informal' ceremony need to be frivolous.

5.7 Which awards should be conferred at the ceremony?

There are two basic factors which may determine whether an institution wishes to confer only degrees at the ceremony, or whether it wishes the ceremony to confer all awards of any type and at any level. For some institutions the decision may be based on concepts of the function of the ceremony and the status of the awards; for others the question may be determined on more practical and less theoretical grounds of how many students can be accommodated in the space available.

The traditions of the institution may themselves implicitly lead it to a position of awarding only degrees at the ceremony. If the institution has a long history of degree-level courses, with only a small number of non-degree awards, the latter may have been made only to students who had not successfully completed the degree originally being studied. Such institutions may subconsciously be regarding these 'fallback' awards as consolation prizes for students who have failed, which therefore have no place at an awards ceremony. This position may be more difficult to defend as the breadth of awards and types becomes ever more complex. However, the institutions may find themselves defending their decision to have 'degree ceremonies' on these grounds when in fact they are being driven to it on grounds of the potential size of the ceremony: the policy of excluding non-degree awards is driven by a desire to keep the ceremonies manageable rather than on questions of principle.

If, on the other hand, the institution has its background in a broader range of courses, with a strong emphasis on certificates, diplomas and other non-degree work, this tradition will be more likely to lead to ceremonies at which the institution's awards at all levels are conferred. To some extent this may have been influenced by a position in which any degrees being awarded were those validated by outside bodies: if such an institution wished to celebrate its own success it will tend to have developed a broader role for its ceremonies, so that locally based certificates and diplomas can be presented in a show of local pride.

An institution finding itself in the latter position will, in an era of hugely increased participation rates, find itself forced along a treadmill of increasingly complex and numerous awards ceremonies.

Separating out the non-degree awards to a different ceremony is not the answer. If the institution is going to have 'degree ceremonies' and 'other awards ceremonies' it is saving very little in terms of the complexity of managing them: it might as well have them in the main one in that case.

There is no right and wrong answer to this question. Those who have 'degree only' ceremonies will be criticized as being elitist by those who have 'comprehensive' ceremonies; and they in turn will be criticized as having ceremonies which look like secondary school prize days by the former (there is nothing wrong with prize days in the right context; the question is whether an awards ceremony *is* the right context). The point is important, as it crucially affects the size and frequency of ceremonies. Each institution must decide its position, on pragmatic grounds as well as on points of principle, and must be willing and able to defend it as it sees fit.

5.8   Can you confer posthumous awards?

The question of posthumous awards is often vexed, so it may be useful to cover it in some detail here. The first point to clarify is the distinction between posthumous awards and aegrotat awards; not all posthumous awards are aegrotats, and not all aegrotat awards are posthumous; some awards may be both posthumous and an aegrotat:

- posthumous awards are those conferred on students who have died;
- aegrotat awards are those based on special evidence when the normal assessment has not been possible for medical reasons.

There have been differing legal viewpoints on whether it is possible to make posthumous awards. One view is that, even if all the examinations have been passed, it is not possible to confer a posthumous award since to do so requires the existence of a person on whom to confer it; once a person is dead, that person no longer exists in legal terms and can, therefore, not receive any further citations of any sort. It should be noted that this view is not based on any questioning of a university's powers, but the legal possibility of doing something for or to a deceased person.

Apparently there is no comparison to be drawn with the awarding of posthumous medals and honours, since the latter are discretionary or earned as the result of a judgement, whereas academic qualifications are earned by virtue of reaching a particular standard or carrying out specific acts. This is a rather subtle argument. Nor is there a parallel with hereditary titles: academic awards are specific to individuals during their lifetimes, and awards and their eligibility die with them.

The alternative view is that, irrespective of whether it is meaningful to try to confer an award on a dead student, no person actually loses anything by the act, and there is considerable compassionate reason to confirm to the student's family what level of achievement the student had reached. As no damage can be done to any person by such an act, there is no risk of legal challenge, and the institution might as well do it if it wishes to.

There are academic questions to be considered when determining whether a posthumous award can be made. Most institutions would agree that a posthumous award can be considered for a student whose death has occurred after all assessments have been made: for example, if the death occurs between the meeting of the board of examiners and the date of conferral. If the assessments have been made but the board of examiners has not yet met, the institution must ensure that these assessments have been marked in the normal way if it is going to consider a posthumous award. If an institution permits the conferral of aegrotat awards (failure to complete due to illness), there would seem to be no academic reason for not considering posthumous awards (failure to complete due to death). It may seem harsh to regard death as merely a severe form of illness, but the academic questions are the same.

If an institution is going to make aegrotat or posthumous awards it is best to treat all processes in exactly the same way as it would for other students. Above all, the institution should resist the temptation to make posthumous or aegrotat awards on compassionate grounds. The standards of the institution's awards must be maintained even where conferred on deceased students; to do otherwise devalues the award conferred on the deceased student, is patronizing to the relatives of the student and does a great disservice to the institution.

Although they have a longer history than posthumous awards, aegrotat awards have not been universally available; in some institutions a poor performance in a key subject could simply mean that the course had been failed; if there was no provision for resits (also a traditional feature) the student's whole period of study was therefore wasted.

5.9   What awards can be made?

There is no legislation on what awards an institution can make: BA, BSc, LLM etc. Every institution can make up its own awards, although professional and (inter)national consistency will need to be respected. This can occasionally cause conflict if there is a national trend towards a designation which is not covered by that institution's own conventions: there can be internal resentment against introducing new awards merely because others have done so, what some managers refer to as 'me-too-ism'. However, failure to do so may lead to the graduates not being regarded as having up-to-date qualifications. New designations are sometimes introduced deliberately (e.g. MBA, DClinPsych), others evolve naturally (BSc, BEng).

It is possibly unwise to have too many different awards, especially if doing so merely repeats information contained in the course title (BPsy, BEng, BEcon, BHist, BEd, BLang, BSoc, BChem, BMath, etc.), unless there is a specific professional need: once the institution has started down this path it will find itself forced to add more and more as each discipline expects the same rights to a distinctive award title.

5.10 What is the role of the brochure for the ceremony?

At first sight it may seem an unimportant matter what the status is of the brochure of names printed and published for an awards ceremony. However, it is important that an institution decides for its own purposes exactly what its status is, as it affects the way in which records are kept.

If the ceremony is a 'conferral' ceremony, it is important that there is a single unambiguous record of which awards have been conferred there. It is almost inevitable, no matter how well managed the arrangements, that sooner or later a discrepancy will arise between what is in the brochure and what happens at the ceremony: there might be a misprint in the brochure, a name may need to be added, a name may need to be deleted, a classification may have been changed following an appeal, etc. Presenters may also make mistakes when reading out the details, giving the wrong course title or classification. Corrections to the brochure may be made orally by the presenter as and when appropriate in the ceremony, or may be made by publishing a supplementary list of addenda and corrigenda.

This raises the question of which version is 'correct': the version as printed or the version as read out. If the argument is that the brochure is definitive unless corrected by the presenter, what is the status of accidental slips made by the presenter? If a course named in the brochure as 'engineering studies' is corrected by the presenter to 'engineering science', and that is enough to legitimise the change, does it mean that if the presenter misreads a correct brochure entry of 'engineering physics' as if it said 'environmental physics', the student actually has a degree in the latter? On the other hand, if a mistake is discovered in the brochure after the ceremony, so that it was not corrected by the presenter, what award or course title has the student got: what the brochure says or what the board of examiners decided?

The answer to this conundrum may sound obvious, but it is basically a fudge. Institutions rarely announce corrections to the brochure in the middle of a ceremony, as it would be too embarrassing, but they ought to do so if they regard the brochure as the official record. The attitude to unspotted mistakes is also often fudged: if a student is accidentally awarded a degree with a lower classification than it should have, the institution usually does the honourable thing and reconfers it (by chair's action – see section 5.2(a)), reissuing the certificate with an apology. If a student is accidentally awarded a degree with a higher classification than it should have, many institutions do not reclaim the issued award, as it would be too difficult to face the legal challenges about the legitimacy of the original mistaken award; a wise institution will inform the student of the mistake and invite the student to return the certificate which bears the incorrect higher award, and advise him or her that an attempt to claim the higher classification would not be substantiated by the marks on the transcript.

It is therefore wise for the administrators of the ceremonies to keep a file copy of the brochure clearly marked up with any changes and mistakes, whether in the text or made by the presenter on the day, so that there is a record in case of possible challenges or appeals. This should be supplemented by a list of late additions which were read out at the ceremony.

If the ceremony is just a celebration it is much easier. There is less pressure for the brochure to be definitive copy, it does not act as the source for the official record of what is conferred, since that is held in the board of examiners (as amended by any subsequent changes); nor is there any need for a supplementary brochure or any need to be anxious about the status of any misreadings made at the ceremony.

One occasionally contentious question is whether the brochure should include mention of the student's honours classification: some regard this as a matter of great importance; others regard it as merely incidental to the award and feel that it is elitist to brand one student as 'better' than another in a publication of this kind.

5.11 What is the role of academic dress?

Formal academic dress can be a matter of great institutional pride, and of much misunderstanding. Originally academic dress was nothing special: that is to say, it formed part of the rich medieval tradition of having specified modes of dress for each profession or occupation. The origins of modern academic dress lie in medieval clerical costumes, which explains the cowl-like hood used in most robes, and the similarity of chancellors' and vice-chancellors' robes to those of the Lord Chancellor in the House of Lords. As with clerical dress, academic gowns were originally worn closed at the front, as is still the case in some institutions in Europe.

Around the sixteenth century, as male clothing became more a statement of fashion, the habit arose of wearing the robes open at the front so that the more richly decorated clothes beneath them could be seen. The addition of colour-coded linings and trimmings, to identify the wearer's status and allegiance, followed shortly afterwards. As universities became more secular, the links with ecclesiastical dress became weaker. Within this context it is no great surprise that a great divergence of practice arose; it should also be clear that there are no 'rules' as to what the particular form of gown for a particular award or institution should be. It is, in the end, a matter for each institution to decide. Many institutions adopt a single colour for all their awards, and indicate the gradation from sub-degree work to doctorate by increasing the proportion or prominence of one of the colours; others have different colours for different subjects; some have fur-trimmed gowns or hoods for particular awards. The scope for difference is enormous.

Is it elitist to wear 'uniforms'? Academic dress has not kept pace with changes in dress habits outside academe. This has led some to regard the wearing of academic dress as a demonstration of elitism. There is no intrinsic reason why this should be so, any more than the wearing of any other uniform is elitist. The formal dress of many uniformed services, such as nursing, is merely a tradition based on the needs for functional clothing suitable for the efficient performance of duties, and for demonstrating your allegiance; in essence it is no more elitist than wearing the strip of your local sports club.

Is it elitist not to give academic dress to diplomas/certificates? An area where there is definite difference of opinion which could be more fairly charged with being elitist is any decision not to permit the wearing of academic dress to students with awards which are not degrees. This is usually closely linked to the decision as to whether the institution will present such awards at its ceremonies (see section 5.7 above). As with academic dress itself, there is no wrong or right answer to this: if an institution wishes to identify and permit the wearing of academic dress for its certificates and diplomas it has every right to do so.

Getting the correct balance between 'elitism' and 'recognition of achievement' is not always easy. It is not unknown for half of the students on a course to be offended that their course does not qualify them to wear academic dress, and then, when the entitlement is added, the other half to be offended that they have to wear 'elitist' robes. In the end the institution simply has to decide for itself, and, if necessary, prepare its rebuttal of charges of elitism from some quarters.

5.12 Charging for attendance ▮

Policies on charging for awards ceremonies vary widely. Some of the possible things for which a charge may be levied are:

- Attendance: some charge for attending, some charge for not attending.
- Buffet: some provide a free buffet for the graduand and all guests, some charge for the guests only, some provide free buffet for the graduate and first two guests only, some do not provide a buffet at all.
- Guest tickets: some make no attendance charge at all, some charge for all guest tickets, some only for extra tickets above a normal minimum (typically two).
- Brochure: some issue the brochure free to all those attending, some issue a basic programme free but charge for a glossy brochure with full names and souvenir articles.

The permutations on the above are many, and there is no standard practice at all. Awards ceremonies are not cheap to arrange and run, but students who have paid large sums to follow their course may be very resentful if the final element is not included in what they have paid. Attendance is in itself an intrinsically costly act, with robe hire, transport, hotels, etc.; to add a charge for actually coming seems to some an unkind act to those who have served the institution well. In the end, the institution must decide on its own balance between cost recovery and public relations; there is no right or wrong answer.

5.13 Awards made *in absentia* ▮

Most (but not all) institutions permit students to receive their awards without attending a ceremony, or to be conferred *in absentia*, as the Latin phrase is used. If the ceremony is a 'celebration' rather than a 'conferral' this is uncontentious, and probably totally irrelevant. Students at those institutions which not only define their ceremony as being the act of conferral, but also refuse to confer awards *in absentia*, in effect never graduate if they do not attend.

Some institutions levy a charge for not coming; most do not as they see it as a way of decreasing pressure on the ceremony itself.

Although some institutions make the students apply formally if they wish to receive their award *in absentia*, many assume that failure to respond to the invitation, or failure to turn up on the day, means that the student wishes to receive the award *in absentia*; the alternative would be to defer them to the next ceremony, which would add complexity to the administration, carrying names forward year after year until they are formally archived as 'unconferred'.

The way in which awards *in absentia* are recognized in the proceedings can vary. At some stage it is wise (though it may not legally be necessary) for an announcement to be made to the effect that 'awards are also conferred on those named in the order of proceedings but not in attendance'. It is probably best not to rely simply on a note in the brochure to this effect (though this may suffice if the brochure is defined as being the authoritative record – see section 5.10). A single announcement at the end of the ceremony should be adequate: it is not necessary to make the announcement after each course.

If an institution requires students to make formal application for an award *in absentia* it can dispense with the above announcement if it marks in the brochure (and announces) each award made *in absentia*. However, it must be very careful how it deals with the case of students who book a place at a ceremony but (for whatever reason) fail to arrive in time. If the institution then makes an award *in absentia* it undermines its requirement for a formal application; if it does not, it might find itself needing to make an announcement at the end of the proceedings informing the assembly about any awards in the brochure which have now not been conferred after all; this can be very messy.

5.14 Who should not be let into the ceremony?

The way in which an institution treats those arriving late for the ceremony is intimately connected with the way in which it treats awards *in absentia* (see section 5.13). Some institutions stop entry 15 minutes before the start so that the readers can have an accurate list of those present; others give the readers a list of all those who intended to come, which means on one hand that there may be embarrassing gaps if a student fails to come after all, but on the other hand there is no need to worry about late arrivals needing to be added to the reader's copy (unless for some reason they are also not in the brochure).

Institutions should not allow students in if their award is being withheld for non-payment: this can only lead to embarrassing scenes. It is up to each institution whether it wishes to retain the right to turn students away at the door if they are improperly dressed; some institutions have very strict criteria for this, others have no regulations at all (although fortunately few students have tested just how far this tolerance will go). If it is a conferral ceremony students should at least be *encouraged* to dress neatly (howsoever defined); at a celebration ceremony an institution may feel it can be more relaxed.

5.15   Who does what at the ceremony?

There are very few formal requirements governing procedures at the ceremony. There will usually be a restriction or requirement concerning who needs to be there to effect the conferral (see section 5.2(a)), but apart from that it is really up to the institution to decide who does what in the ceremony itself.

Reading out the names. Some institutions have individuals with particularly good voice projection who will read out every name; some institutions invite each Dean to read out the names of all the students in that faculty; some use the tutor in charge of the course in question to read out the names for each course. It may even be the academic registrar or other administrator. Provided that the names are read out competently and clearly the choice of person does not matter.

Conferring the award. Many institutions include a physical act which symbolizes the moment of conferral. This is a relic of the 'laying on of hands' implicit in a religious ceremony such as that described in section 5.1. In modern times the most common act is a simple handshake; this may be given by the officiating officer (for example, the vice-chancellor), or may be the dean of the faculty (assuming that the dean is not busy reading out the names). Some institutions with long histories have developed local rituals with little obvious function: the utterance of particular words, touching particular items of clothing, being touched by the chancellor's hat etc. These have no legal function, but do no harm except to those who would reduce all ceremonies to the same formal structure: a little whimsy is no bad thing in these circumstances, and most rituals have a very flimsy basis if analysed too closely. No physical act is strictly necessary, but as a symbol of the transition from 'graduand' to 'graduate' it can be a very effective identifiable point in the ceremony.

Care must be taken not to require the more arcane elements if they will conflict with a student's ethical or religious beliefs: some students may be forbidden by their beliefs from touching others, or from confirming allegiance to particular tenets or faiths. At the very least, the institution must inform students of any such practices and offer them an alternative formulation.

5.16   Where do you hold the ceremonies?   ■

Institutions often do not have much choice about the location of their ceremonies. To a certain extent the choice (if there is one) may be governed by the institution's decision as to the style and function of the ceremony.

(a) Cathedrals

A very common venue is the local cathedral. This may be a relic of the ecclesiastical origins of the ceremony, but is now mainly used because it is a very attractive venue for students and parents, and probably has a usefully large capacity. In the United Kingdom this will tend to be a Christian cathedral, but (perhaps to the surprise of some) there appear to be very few objections from non-Christian students to attending these venues: possibly their reservations manifest themselves by absence rather than by complaint. There is usually little that an institution can do about this if there is no alternative accommodation.

There is more likely to be a problem for cathedrals when, in times of rapidly increasing student participation, the number of ceremonies also increases and cathedrals find it very difficult to make block bookings for a whole week or more. There may also be restrictions on when a cathedral will be available in the year, and some of them are reluctant to be closed at what can be a peak time for tourists or religious festivals. Even if these constraints can be overcome, the institution must still expect to be asked to work around the regular practices of the cathedral in terms of services: typically this involves guaranteeing to have finished by a particular time in the late afternoon. In rare cases the cathedral may simply not be available at the required time.

Although cathedrals may have been designed for mass attendance at religious ceremonies, they are not always flexible for the needs of awards ceremonies. There may be excellent organs to play the music for the processions, but the acoustics for speech are not always good, the buildings may be cold (which is sometimes a positive feature for summer ceremonies), pillars may obstruct the view for many of those present and the seating may need to be set up each morning and dismantled each afternoon if there are evening activities with different needs.

Last but not least, higher education institutions are not necessarily built near to cathedrals, so that complicated arrangements may be needed to transport students, staff and guests between the cathedral and the institution.

(b) Civic halls

Large civic halls share some of the drawbacks of cathedrals, and although they may have better heating than some cathedrals, they also tend to cost more to hire. They have a greater tendency to be unavailable if there is the chance of a lucrative long-term booking. If the hall is a concert hall the acoustics may be better, but the seating tends not to be conducive to easy processing of students to the stage and back for their conferral.

(c) Institutional halls

Some institutions are fortunate enough to have a large main hall of their own. If these are large enough, and smart enough, they offer significant advantages over externally hired halls: they add a splendid feeling of local warmth and pride, and the logistics for the graduates and guests are considerably simplified. The feeling gained by going straight from the ceremony to strawberries and cream on the lawn outside is far better than that obtained from being ferried by fleets of buses from the town centre back to the campus. The halls may not, though, have the facilities for such grand processional music as cathedrals and civic halls unless they have also been equipped as concert halls, and the use of games halls is probably best avoided if the normal, routine use cannot be effectively disguised.

5.17 The number of ceremonies

The number of ceremonies is a matter of local choice, and is a function of the size of available rooms and the time available; in these factors many institutions have little choice. The choice is effectively only between having many small ceremonies and having fewer but larger ceremonies. Having a few large ceremonies is more demanding on the stamina of the administrators, but having a large number of smaller ceremonies can be exceedingly tedious if the same support staff are involved in all, not to mention if the vice-chancellor or principal has to give the same speech at each one.

5.18 Guests

Apart from their constitutional conferral function, the main purpose of awards ceremonies is to round off students' studies in a pleasant way for the graduates and their relatives and friends. The choice of venue, and the decision as to the number of ceremonies, can have an effect on the number of spare seats left for guests. If one of the main functions of the ceremony is to reward the graduate by holding a splendid ceremony, it can be marred if there are tight restrictions on the number of guests who can attend. This is particularly the case if the student is from another country, where it is very common for the family of the student to wish to come to the ceremony in quite large numbers – parents, children, grandparents, aunts, uncles, etc. If the institution has few constraints on the number of ceremonies, it might wish to take into account the number of guest tickets which will be made available by having a larger number of ceremonies. Restricting guest tickets to just two per graduate may be particularly harsh for mature students, who could have to choose between bringing their partner and children or their parents.

5.19 Who should be in the procession?

If there is going to be a ceremony, the institution will normally want to have some sort of act to open it: this will typically be a procession of some sort, though this does not imply that it needs to be particularly formal. If the institution has a mace this is a good time to use it: it should go at the front of the procession both on entering and on leaving, since historically it had the potential function of clearing the way of obstructing bodies.

If the ceremony is being held in a civic hall the council may wish the civic mace bearer to process too: local convention determines which should precede the other, depending among other things on perceptions of who is the host and who the guest. In some cases there may be other civic officers, such as beadles or sword bearers; the presence of these may depend on whether the mayor is in attendance.

If the ceremony is in a cathedral there may be a desire on the cathedral's part for a verger or other officer to lead the procession. Often this is only as far as the door of the cathedral, although local rules differ.

The main procession will normally consist of the senior academic officers of the institution (chancellor, vice-chancellor, etc.), and a selection of academic staff. If there is more than one ceremony, the academic staff will often be those closely involved with the courses whose awards are being conferred. Custom and practice varies as to the relative order of people in the procession: some process in ascending seniority (chancellor at the rear), some in descending seniority (chancellor at the fore). Normally the order is reversed when leaving, although this is likely to be based on the ease of lining people up rather than on any particular theory of precedence.

Just a note on what constitutes a mace: in the days of armoured personal battle, bishops were not permitted to use a sword since that might break any oath not to shed blood – crushing and maiming appeared more acceptable, even if equally fatal. As these maces joined the swords in ceremonial use, the original spikes were dropped and the handle became more ornamental. The result was that in order to keep their balance, the bearers tended to carry them with the heavy end (formerly the handle) over one shoulder and the easier end (formerly the functional end) at the bottom. Maces come in a variety of lengths: those which are longer and thinner with a less bulky handle are better referred to as a 'stave', leaving 'mace' to describe those which are shorter with a bulkier handle.

5.20 What is the role of Honorary graduates and fellowships?

Honorary awards are made when an institution wishes to recognize people of note by suggesting that their achievements are of a standard equivalent to those of the institution's awards. If the achievement is not in an academic field, institutions can also confer fellowships or life memberships: these are typically 'for services to the institution', though honorary masters degrees are also often used for this purpose.

Practices differ on who may be considered for an honorary award. Some institutions restrict their honorary awards to those who have had links with the institution itself; others feel that they can give honours to local, national and international figures. In some cases this can be used as a means of publicizing the institution, particularly if the award is made to an eminent figure in a discipline in which the institution feels it has great strength. Some institutions see benefit in making awards to celebrities for achievements which have little if any academic content but which may none the less be very worthy: contributions to charity, for example. There is no reason why they should not choose to do so if they wish, though there is a risk attached to using this power excessively as it can detract from the dignity of the awards themselves and may offend other recipients.

There is little if any legislation covering honorary awards, and many of the points made above about awards therefore do not apply. There seems little point in conferring them posthumously without opening up a huge (and fascinating) field of potential recipients.

Certainly they can be conferred *in absentia* (for example, if the recipient is taken ill at the last minute).

When awards ceremonies were relatively small affairs it was common to make one or more awards at each ceremony. The growth in student numbers and ceremonies presents a challenge to this: if the institution continues to make an award at each ceremony it may run out of worthy recipients; if it does not it may deprive a long ceremony of a natural break in the middle, which can relieve the audience from what can be a very uninteresting recital of names.

Honorary awards are given for a reason. It makes sense to inform those present what this reason is. This should be included in summary form in the ceremony brochure, but this is normally supplemented by a more extensive oration or eulogy of some sort. It does not matter who gives the oration: it can be the vice-chancellor, or whoever nominated the recipient, or any member of staff who has good voice projection. Some institutions ask recipients to reply with a speech of their own; some do not. It is nice, however, if there is some sort of symbolic act to complete the conferral: the recipient may be publicly decked in the robes, or may be summoned from the body of the audience to take his or her place in the platform party. The institution may also take this opportunity for a ceremonial signing of a book of honours. As well as having ceremonial value, such a book forms a handy record of recipients over the years.

One question often asked by those receiving honorary awards concerns their status. It is normal *not* to mention one's honorary awards on letterheads or visiting cards; in biographies or directories they should be listed separately and identified. They should certainly not be used in a way which implies that they have academic validity (for example, in job applications), otherwise there may be subsequent accusations of misleading the employers.

5.21 Certificates ■

Certificate design and format is very much a matter of local taste, ranging from the bland to the gaudy. The only real point of issue which arises is when there is a difference of opinion about the student's name, or, more often, the way in which the name is presented. This is most often an issue with students from countries which do not use the 'English' order of names: for example, those where the family name comes first (as in Chinese), or where there is part of a family name not normally used as such (as in Spanish or Icelandic).

If the ceremony is a conferral event, it is very important that the name shown in the brochure has exactly the same format, spelling and order as it does on the certificate; if this is not insisted upon, there is the risk of problems later if verification of a certificate is required. The format of the name should be checked with the student during their final year, to avoid misunderstandings. Just as common are the issues arising from students whose name changes between the award and the conferral, typically as the result of marriage. If the institution wishes, it can confer the certificate under the new name and add an endorsement to the rear confirming how the student was known during the course.

If a replacement certificate is requested showing a married name, or a name changed by deed poll, it is best to put the new name on the main part of the certificate and add an endorsement on the rear stating 'original conferred under name XYZ', with the full name. Some institutions prefer to do this the other way round, adding an endorsement to the rear of the certificate stating that 'the person shown overleaf is now known as XYZ'. On the rare occasions where these approaches might be felt insensitive – for example, where the student studied as one sex and now lives as the other – the best solution is to reissue the certificate as above, with the new full name, but just give initials in the endorsement on the rear rather than the full names (which could cause embarrassment).

5.22 Who is it all for?

It must be remembered that the main point of the ceremony is for the students and their guests, not for the institution. However, it is important too for the institutional psychology to see its successes paraded as people, rather than as names and forms. It can increase the institution's self-confidence and corporate awareness. It is also probably the only time when staff see all the students happy; this is particularly rewarding for those administrative and managerial staff who only meet students when they are in difficulties. In the end, it should be a memorable occasion for all those attending.

6

DISCIPLINE

The need for discipline, whether Adam Smith was right, and the scope of discipline and sanctions.

Unruly children make their sire stoop with oppression.
(William Shakespeare, *Richard II*, III.iv.30)

Who can control.
(William Shakespeare, *Othello*, V.ii.264)

We must regulate all recreations and pastimes.
(John Milton, *Areopagitica*)

6.1 The reason for disciplinary procedures

Over 200 years ago, in 1776, Adam Smith wrote in *The Wealth of Nations* that 'The discipline of colleges and universities is in general contrived, not for the benefit of the students, but for the interest, or more properly speaking, for the ease of the masters' (V.i.f.15). (*Series Editors' comment*: this is another example of what Shaw called 'conspiracies against the laity'.) This may be a rather cynical view of the role of disciplinary procedures in educational institutions. However, if one were to substitute 'institution' for 'masters' it would not be far from the truth.

As with most disciplinary procedures, whether in education, the armed forces, other closed orders or society in general, the aim is to curtail personal excesses which impinge on the rights of others. The skill comes in balancing the long traditions of academic freedom with the need to prevent the abuse of this freedom by a small number bent on exploiting it to their personal advantage at the expense of others. The clearest example of this balancing act is the question of freedom of speech and academic freedom in general: the desire to hear and examine all points of view often conflicts with a desire to suppress those views which society at large regards as offensive (e.g. racism). What makes this balance even more difficult to achieve is that higher education institutions are at the same time 'private' bodies, yet open to public access and scrutiny: what an institution may wish to permit within its walls in the interests of open debate may be misunderstood or misrepresented by those outside as a licence to express extreme views.

These present notes do not, of course, cover staff discipline, which is heavily circumscribed by employment law. They attempt instead to cover some of the general points arising from student discipline. More detailed comments are included in other chapters on the sort of things which students get up to which need disciplinary action in connection with examinations (see Chapter 4), attendance (Chapter 7) and recruitment (see Chapter 2); Chapter 8 also examines the impact of the law on some of these processes, such as certificate fraud and debt.

6.2 Academic or behavioural? ▊

There are two areas of activity in which an institution may wish to exercise control over its students. The first may be described as 'academic discipline', and covers things like cheating and other attempts to subvert the institutional processes to achieve a status or award to which a student is not entitled; the approach to these may differ widely from one institution to another, and may well raise questions which do not arise outside education. The second may be described as 'behavioural', and covers general misdeeds to which students, being human beings, are as prone as any other members of society: for example, theft, assault, racism or improper car parking.

The distinction between the two types of misdemeanour described above is often (but not always) reflected in the way the regulations and procedures on discipline are managed within institutions. It is fairly common for procedures connected with academic discipline (cheating, impersonation, etc.) to be handled within the student administration registry, whereas the behavioural discipline would be handled by the institution's legal experts, since it may sometimes be necessary to involve the police or the courts.

However, the distinction between the two is sometimes not as clear as described above. Institutions must always try to have a clear definition of what sort of misdemeanour falls into which category, and also which misdeeds can be handled by internal procedures and which should be handed over to the police. The regulations must avoid any ambivalence which could be misinterpreted as an attempt to conceal within internal procedures an act which should have been handed over to external agencies. For example, sexual harassment could be used to gain an advantage in examination marking or continuous assessment, but should not be treated merely as 'cheating'. Misuse of drugs may need to be considered as a matter for reporting to the police rather than just internal discipline. Faking the qualifications on a certificate may be treated as a local disciplinary matter, whereas an outside agency issuing a bogus certificate may need to be pursued through the courts (see further section 6.8).

Some minor disciplinary procedures may be best handled at the departmental level. This is not just acts related to local procedures such as payment for photocopies, but also things which are best monitored locally, such as absenteeism. There should, however, be a threshold for deciding when the main central disciplinary procedures should take over, e.g. when late payment for materials becomes a formal institutional debt, or casual absenteeism becomes a reason for the termination of enrolment.

6.3   Role of Vice-Chancellor or Principal

Whatever the powers exercised by the bodies mentioned in section 6.2, they are all ultimately acting on behalf of the supreme body of the institution (the academic board, senate, board of governors, etc.), as it is in the latter that the powers are usually vested by the statutes or charter of the institution. For this reason the disciplinary bodies usually act with powers delegated to them from the higher committees, and often have to make a formal recommendation to them before the outcomes and sanctions can be agreed and implemented. This, in turn, means that appeals against any outcomes will normally ultimately rest with the chancellor, vice-chancellor or principal, in their capacity as chair of that body.

6.4   Who should constitute the panel?

Panels for disciplinary hearings usually comprise a mixture of academic staff who are highly experienced in the regulations and workings of the institution, and those who have a proven record of concern for student welfare. In fortunate cases these need not be different people. The different roles are important: it is crucial that the regulations and powers are always exercised with scrupulous care and consistency, but also that they are exercised with full sympathy for the plight of the students before them.

Although there is no legal requirement to do so, many institutions include one or more students on the disciplinary panels. The benefits of this are twofold: first, it can help to ensure the second dimension of disciplinary hearings mentioned above; second, it can ensure that the procedures have the confidence of the student community. Typically the student member can be one of the officers of the students union or similar body; this has the advantage that such officers (whether in sabbatical roles or not) are fairly well informed on procedural matters. If this is the case, however, they must appreciate that they are not on the panel to represent the student's own view, or to act as 'counsel for the defence'.

6.5 Central and local powers

As well as the central disciplinary powers and committees mentioned above, there is often considerable scope for formal disciplinary powers to be exercised at the local departmental level. This applies to both academic and support departments. Most institutions have regulations which govern behaviour in libraries, on computer systems or in residences, and it is quite common for misuse of such facilities to be dealt with by the manager of the facility through suspension of privileges, levying of small fines or temporary withdrawal of some access facilities. If this is the case the sanctions which can be imposed should not be so draconian as to affect the student's academic progress or status: penalties of that severity should be reserved for the formal central committees and powers.

Whether the disciplinary powers are exercised locally or centrally, the same basic rules of natural justice ('due process' in US legal terminology) should apply, which are that the students must know the full nature of the charges against them, and should have the right to present evidence to a hearing. It is important to note that 'natural justice' does not necessarily mean that there has to be the right to a hearing *in person*; evidence and defence in writing meets these needs too. This concept can become quite important when students turn down the invitation to appear before the disciplinary committee: by doing so they must not be able to invalidate or postpone indefinitely the procedures or sanctions available to the committee. If the student fails to attend despite adequate notice the committee can hear the case in their absence, as indeed it can if the student declines to present a defence; none the less it is vital that the power to do this is explicitly declared in the regulations and procedures.

There is a natural tendency, which must be resisted, to view local disciplinary powers and procedures as somehow 'lighter' than central procedures. Certainly they can be softer in terms of the trauma inflicted on the students, but that must not be accompanied by any loss of rigour, or of fairness. Discretion to exercise local powers must not be seen as a quick and painless way of dealing with cases for which there is insufficient evidence for a formal panel. The choice between local and central discipline must rest solely on the severity of the misdeed, not upon the strength of the evidence. This question arises most clearly in cases of plagiarism in coursework: the department may have every reason, from its knowledge of the student, to suspect that the submitted piece of work is not theirs but is copied from other sources or other students. There is a strong temptation in such cases for the department simply to challenge the student by giving a mark of zero on the assumption that the work is plagiarized, and seeing if they appeal. This is not satisfactory justice even though the outcome may be appropriate: the ends do not justify the means, and an appeal by the student would probably succeed. This can be *immensely* frustrating for the tutorial staff and administration alike, just as it is outside academia when known criminals are found not guilty of crimes which all parties know they have committed, because the evidence is inconclusive; educational institutions are not exempt from the rules of evidence, but, fortunately for them, the burden of proof is more akin to that in civil litigation rather than the higher standard required for criminal prosecution in the courts.

6.6 Penalties

The penalties must be proportionate to the offence. This is not just a question of fairness, but also of reducing the likelihood of appeals. The same applies whether the penalty is financial or academic. Small debts may have no actual sanction until the student tries to re-enrol the next year or to receive the award, whereas large debts (particularly for tuition fees) may result in instant termination of enrolment. Fines for non-academic misdeeds such as parking violations, smoking in residences or damaging library books should not be so high that the student's enrolment is jeopardized; unless, that is, the parking were in the vice-chancellor's office, the smoking was deliberately to set off the fire alarms or the library books were deliberately vandalized in a gross or large-scale way. For minor plagiarism a mark of zero on that piece of work might be appropriate; for blatant cheating or bribery in examinations expulsion might be appropriate. As can be seen, the range of offences within any one category can be wide, so the range of penalties must be commensurately wide.

The penalties must also be timely: a penalty for a serious offence which does not come into effect until the next year's enrolment may be perceived as weak by the student community. Penalties which are contingent on there being no second offence (fairly common with minor cheating) may be perceived as giving students one free attempt at the offence. This, in the context of cheating, can be most damaging, as it is almost an invitation to keep on cheating until caught, and then be let off with only a warning if it is the first proved offence. Similarly, the penalty for non-payment of a disciplinary fine ought to be treated more severely than other debts, since it is a flouting of the disciplinary action itself.

Whatever the penalty, it must be covered in the regulations concerned, or within the normal reasonable scope of any discretion allowed (see Chapter 8, section 8.8, for further discussion of the role of 'reasonable' decisions). The nature of the penalty should also be related to the nature of the offence: non-academic offences should not affect a student's marks directly, nor would it be common to apply fines for cheating without an academic penalty in addition (otherwise the rich students could cheat more freely than the poor ones). However, it is perfectly legitimate for an academic penalty to affect work other than that on which the offence was committed: blatant cheating on one module can often lead to the student being given a lower award or classification even if the marks themselves still suggest a higher one. This is useful if the institution wants to ensure that a student who cheats on a piece of work ends up with a harsher outcome than a weak student who simply fails it. Such procedures are legitimate if they are expressly allowed for in the regulations and are considered and carried out properly (see Chapter 8, section 8.12, on judicial reviews).

6.7 Withholding of information, awards and enrolment as a sanction

It may sound unlikely that an institution may wish, as a sanction for an infringement of regulations, to withhold information from the student, but this does happen. The most frequent instances concern debts. Very often the main sanction which an institution has against a student with unpaid fees is to withhold their examination results. There are two strings to this:

- the student will presumably be very keen to find out the results, giving an incentive to clear the debts;

• telling the student that he or she has failed is more likely to see the disappearance of the student than the ultimate settling of the debt.

Withholding such information is relatively straightforward with manual records, and does not complicate routine procedures such as mark processing – all that is needed is to process everything as normal except for issuing the results. For computerized records this may be made more complicated by the ability of the student to demand to see their data under access rights enshrined in data protection legislation (see Chapter 9); trying to circumvent the legislation means abandoning computerized systems for a single student, which can add considerably to the normal processes.

It is more straightforward when considering withholding an award at the end of the course. Even if students know that they have passed the course completely, the institution can still refuse to confer the award, in which case the students cannot claim to have obtained it (see Chapter 5, section 5.2(a)). Requests for references and transcripts can state, openly and fairly, that the award has not been conferred (although a potential employer requesting such a reference does not have an automatic right to know the reasons for non-conferral). Such a withholding of the final award is fair in the case of failure to pay tuition fees, since it is part of whatever is deemed to be the formal contract with the student. For other fees (such as residence charges) the institution must make it clear in its regulations and procedures that *any* debt to the institution will result in the award being withheld; in fact it is prudent to make such a provision not only for debt but for the retention of any property belonging to the institution, such as library books or computing and laboratory equipment. See further in Chapter 8.

Although for most minor purposes (debt, etc.) an institution will let a student complete the current period of study, but debar them from enrolling on the next one, there are clearly cases where the disciplinary sanction can be immediate suspension from the course, or permanent expulsion. Institutions have this right, provided that it is in their regulations and procedures to do so. At least, this is the case where the offence is related to the person's status as a student, i.e. on academic grounds, incurring institution-related discipline. What needs greater care is taking disciplinary action of any kind against students for misdeeds undertaken outside their student life. Most institutions will have within their disciplinary regulations an offence such as 'bringing the institution into disrepute', which can be used where appropriate if the student commits a serious crime. This should be used with care, however, and legal advice is probably prudent in many cases; otherwise the student could appeal against the sanction on the grounds that his or her offence was not against the institution itself.

6.8 Fraud

Disciplinary action against students proved to have committed fraud in their role as a student should be dealt with very severely, as it is not only a deliberate attempt to subvert the institutional procedures to gain an unfair and unearned advantage, but is also potentially an offence against all other students if it means that the institution's awards fall into disrepute because of the clearly weak students who hold them. Fraud in connection with admission should be punished by expulsion (see Chapter 2); it is a breach of the terms of the offer and contract. Fraud in connection with examinations is equally severe and expulsion should be considered; this applies both to the examinations themselves and to ancillary procedures such as medical notes ostensibly mitigating poor performance (see Chapter 4 on examinations and Chapter 8 on legal issues). Fraud against students who fake certificates and transcripts should be treated severely; action against non-students issuing bogus certificates needs to be pursued through the courts if necessary (see Chapter 8).

6.9 Attendance

Disciplinary action for non-attendance is not all that frequent in many institutions unless attendance is a statutory requirement (see Chapter 7, section 7.5), the view being held that if students wish to waste their time and money by not attending, that is their choice and their responsibility. As long as attendance is not a statutory requirement for government funding, this attitude will prevail.

6.10 Partner colleges

The lines of responsibility for discipline can become blurred when a course is run in partnership with another college. The scope of each institution's powers should be defined in the agreement. For example, infringements of the academic regulations (cheating, absenteeism, debt) may be handled under the regulations and powers of the parent institution, but behavioural misdemeanours (car parking, etc., as mentioned above) would normally be handled by the institution where the student is being taught, or rather where the offence was committed. A student at a partner college should not have the right to appeal to the parent institution on matters of local jurisdiction: not only would that give students on such a course extra rights compared to students on other courses at that institution, but it would also seriously undermine the relationship of the two institutions if one could overrule the other. Certainly the parent institution may be asked to check that the terms of the agreement between the institutions have been followed properly, but that puts the parent institution in the role of a judge holding a judicial review rather than as a court of further appeal (see Palfreyman and Warner 1998, on franchising).

7

RECORDS AND TRANSCRIPTS

How far records are controlled by structures, attendance, and what should be said in transcripts

All trivial fond records, all saws of books, all forms.
(William Shakespeare, *Hamlet*, I.iv.99)

7.1 Models

It is not simply the format of student records which has changed in the past few decades: it is their very function. The record of a student's academic life is not simply a reference tool to assist tutors and provide adequate information for the boards of examiners. The record, or rather the corpus of all the student records, is a management tool, used for planning, marketing, quality control, 'league tables' and all the other multifarious statistics without which modern educational institutions feel they are not properly run.

Traditional methods of manual recording were no longer flexible enough for these modern challenges; fortunately the arrival of sophisticated computerized record systems provided the necessary flexibility for this (although it is tempting to feel that it was the other way round: that the demand for such statistics arose simply because they could be produced). Similarly, the capabilities of such computerized records systems facilitated (encouraged?) more flexible course structures. Current structures are very varied (see Chapter 3), and place differing demands on the accompanying record systems; it is helpful to the efficient (and cost-effective) management of such systems if the variations do not occur too much or too frequently.

Records systems can be set up in many ways. Most systems are set up as computer databases. The factors to be used in determining the best hardware and software to use are not discussed further in this book, as the information technology available evolves so rapidly that guidelines issued one year can be completely out of date before the next.

The best systems can provide a view of the record from a variety of angles. The main elements of student administration need views at the course level, the module/unit level and the student level. If course structures are fairly rigid, a course-based record is often adequate; in a heavily modularized scheme a student-based record will be needed, and will be the only sensible way of organizing it if students are on courses which can be spread over an indeterminate period (see Chapter 3). This raises particular issues for programme validation (see section 7.4).

Meeting all the internal needs for records is unfortunately only part of the story. Government-funded institutions are required to submit statistical returns at regular intervals, often more than once a year. Institutions have no control over the content or format of these returns; this matters little if the information sought is compatible with what the institutions would be collecting anyway, but that is not always the case. These agencies can classify courses and students in a way which does not meet internal needs: for example, a simplistic categorization of 'undergraduate' and 'postgraduate' (see Chapter 3, section 3.5) or ill-defined use of the terms 'full-time' and 'part-time'. If statutory agencies categorize information in a way which is less detailed than internal needs, this can be dealt with by merging internal codes before submitting the returns; when the difference is the other way, and the agency demands data in a more detailed way than is needed internally, the institution will find that it has to undertake work for which it has no use, purely to meet the needs of the statistical returns. This, together with the tendency of these agencies to change the definitions each year, is an unwelcome burden. Sometimes the agencies themselves have no choice but to make the changes, as they have to comply with the demands of the government, and must change definitions and categories in the light of court cases (for example, if a race relations case, unrelated to education, causes a reclassification of ethnic groups). Each of these changes requires corresponding recoding of significant parts of the record system, often only to be changed again the following year.

Funding agencies also affect the way in which records are managed, or categories are coded, if policy is changed on how an institution's students are to be funded: for example, by head-count, by full-time equivalence, by mode of study, by subject-area of the course studied or modules studied. Whole structures can be built up within institutions to deal with funding categories which simply disappear the next year. All these repeated changes not only affect the way in which records are managed (reprogramming, training, revised documentation, etc.), but also use up significant amounts of staff time which could be better spent on actually educating students.

7.2 Who are the records for, and who manages them? ■

As mentioned above, the reasons for having the records themselves can be varied: they can (and should) serve the needs of the institution, the government, statutory agencies, the academic and support departments and, last but not least, the individual students. Addressing these differing (and sometimes conflicting) demands affects the way the maintenance of the records is organized, and who is responsible for ensuring their accuracy. The best systems ensure that those who need to rely on the data are also those responsible for ensuring the accuracy of the data: it is of little use if, for example, entry of student fee information is a low priority for that part of the institution which enters it, or if, on the other hand, tutors who need accurate course and module lists feel that it is not their responsibility to take registers of attendance. This 'ownership' of the data is crucial. The best 'owners' of the data are the students themselves – they have most to lose if their records are wrong, and ought to be placed in a position not only to change any inaccurate data easily but also to be required to ensure that they are changed.

Conceptual 'ownership' of the data is not only a matter of defining who is responsible for their update, it is intimately intertwined with the managerial structure of the institution. Centralized administrations can appear remote and unsympathetic to the needs of students; and also sometimes to departmental academic and administrative staff. Certainly they can appear intimidating to students in a way that departmental staff do not. This is not a question of attitude, more a matter of familiarity, since students have much greater interaction with local office staff. The importance of this is considerable when it comes to making the students feel that they have ownership of the data about them. If the students feel that the only reason for keeping their data up to date is to satisfy 'the centre', there is no incentive to do so; if they feel that they are causing problems for the administrative staff whom they meet every day they may try harder.

The main message to get over to students is that they are responsible for ensuring that the data about them on the system are correct. This does not just mean things which only they know, such as their current address, but all data. The essence of ensuring that data on students are correct is to give the students the responsibility for their accuracy. This involves frequent interaction with them on matters such as addresses, syllabus/modules, coursework marks, attendance records etc.

The question which this in turn raises is whether students should have the ability to change records themselves. For academic questions the answer must remain 'no', but it is less clear that this should be prohibited for personal items such as home and term addresses; unfortunately, acknowledging the temptations of human nature, the answer must still be 'no' even for these, in case there was an inclination to change the address to somewhere inaccurate just before the invoices for fees are due to be processed. The best approach is to give students access to almost all their records, preferably on-line, to make it easy for them to question them and have them corrected and above all to accept that if they do not do so they cannot complain or appeal if incorrect decisions are based on the faulty data which they should have checked. Placing this responsibility on students increases their feeling of 'ownership' of the data, and thereby should increase accuracy, to the mutual benefit of the students and the institution itself.

So the needs of the three constituents of the institution are different:

- students need to be sure that they get the correct result for their course;
- departments need to manage tutorial groups, essay deadlines, work placements, careers information, sickness and attendance (many of the items needed by departments are ephemeral or of short-term relevance only);
- central administration has to ensure that statutory returns are accurate and timely, management information is secure and comprehensive, and resources are correctly and fairly distributed to the departments.

7.3 What goes in the records?

There have been many attempts to devise or impose a standard format for student records on all institutions. Some have been government initiatives, some have been local collaborations, some have been attempts by an institution or commercial body which keenly believes that its internal solution will apply to all others. All appear to be ill-fated. External factors such as statistical agencies do indeed impose a high level of consistency on what the records systems must produce, but they cannot force institutions to arrive at these data in the same way. All institutions, whether universities or colleges, have a high degree of autonomy about their management and administration, which in turn determines how their records will be structured. To expect many institutions to be able to use identical records management systems simply because their 'business' is the same is like expecting all high-street stores to use the same personnel software simply because they operate in similar ways and have to submit the same sort of tax returns.

The statistical agencies will determine many of the fields on the records, and many of the coding values for those fields (although, as noted in section 7.1, this does not rule out institutions having more detailed codes if they wish, provided they are easily mapped on to the statutory values). Within this framework, however, the precise needs will vary from institution to institution, from course to course and from year to year, especially as the statutory agencies change their requirements each year.

For this reason this book will not discuss in detail what information should be stored in records. However, one point which has long been traditional must be questioned in the context of changing course structures and funding methods: the concept of 'course' itself (see Chapter 3). Many statutory and funding returns depend upon a concept of 'what course the student was on this year', which presupposes a normal pattern of full-time study registered for a particular named course; a student's financial support can depend on rather arbitrary definitions of mode of study and course.

Even the concept of 'successful completion' is vague in a system of continuous educational updating. Records may have to be kept live for as long as a student retains the eligibility to resume studies again in a later stage in the course or in an updating 'top-up' course. This is not entirely a new phenomenon, as some professions have a long tradition of continuous professional updating, but modular schemes encourage it in a much wider way.

Because of this, courses and their records may have to be structured in a way which is not necessary for the institution, merely to fit in with reporting requirements. Some statistical returns do not cope well with fully modularized schemes, systems which facilitate or even encourage 'bridges and ladders' between pathways and stages of a programme. Even traditional methods of record keeping can be ill-fitted and cumbersome for these features.

7.4 Programme validation

A key consequence of the factors described above is that it makes it virtually impossible for records systems to check an individual student's programme of modules/units to make sure it is a valid set of studies for the qualification for which they are aiming. In traditional, relatively fixed courses this was easy; the more a structure approaches a fully modular scheme the less meaningful this becomes.

This does not mean that students cannot expect assistance in devising programmes of study which will lead them towards the award which they seek: it merely becomes more complicated. Indeed, such validation is actually more important in a flexible structure, to avoid students reaching the end of their studies only to find that they have missed out a key component and end up with a different award from that which they expected, or with no award at all.

There are two basic ways of approaching this, each of which is feasible but demanding in terms of maintenance of records on course and module structures:

(a) Which modules do I need for this course title?

Students aiming for a particular named award can be told which modules they need to have passed and how that is traced back through prerequisites to map out the mandatory modules for each year of study; the remainder of the study programme can then be filled out with other modules according to the student's own taste. This is comparatively easy to implement on a computerized system, as it starts from a well defined datum (course title) and works back through prerequisites.

(b) Which course title will my modules make me eligible for?

Students choose a range of modules in subjects to which they feel attracted, and ask which awards this could lead to. This can be quite complex to implement, since it means searching the whole database of course structures to see which of them are compatible with the students' declared choice of subjects: such 'what if?' programming can become unmanageable if the declared modules are too few or too general (as all courses in the institution would be listed as 'available'), but if they are part of an iterative process they can be immensely valuable in helping students to construct their programme of study.

7.5 Attendance monitoring

Every institution, and every module and course tutor, needs to know which enrolled students are actually still attending. This is true irrespective of the way in which students are funded, as long as there is still a charge for attendance. Government funding requires confirmation that a student is still attending, and where students are liable for their own fees the institution will need to know how much to charge for. Tutors and departmental administrators need to know a student's attendance so that, if they have dropped out, the schedules of the tutorials, seminars and coursework can be adjusted. Some professional bodies also require strict monitoring of attendance on their courses, especially those where attendance at practical sessions is deemed to be part of demonstrating competence in necessary skills or exposure to key practices. Sponsors also expect that those for whom they are paying are actually attending.

Few institutions can afford the infrastructure involved in manually taking registers at every class on every day; in any case this can be perceived as very 'schoolish' and patronizing to students, especially in higher education. The alternatives include:

- regular sampling (daily, weekly, termly);
- termly signing on;
- passive monitoring.

Passive monitoring has become increasingly feasible under the widespread use of electronic means of controlling access or use of facilities. It may be impractical, though not technologically impossible, to record the attendance of each student in a class (which also raises Orwellian overtones), but it is certainly possible to draw together all instances where a student has interacted in any way with computer systems: use of the library, access to controlled laboratories, use of IT facilities, use of careers software, use of other networked software of systems, etc. If every log-on or access control is logged it becomes easier for an institution to confirm the student's last known date of doing student-related activities. This may not go as far as attesting to activity on a particular module unless coursework submission is electronically logged or particular software is linked to specific modules.

A beneficial side-effect of regular attendance monitoring (whether active or passive) is that it can help an institution to check on possible student problems before the student is able to raise them directly. Many tutors will be aware of occasions where exploring why a student has missed a couple of lectures has uncovered serious personal issues which the student was reluctant to raise; this in turn can enable prompt remedial action to rescue the student's studies.

7.6 Partner colleges

Record keeping on courses run between two institutions in partnership does not usually present problems, but can require careful negotiation and precise agreements on who collects, maintains and updates the records. If a course is run as a 'franchise' then the parent institution will need to collect exactly the same information on partner college students as it does on students based in the institution itself. The franchisee institution will also need to collect and maintain the records which it needs for its own purposes. In turn, the partner college will need appropriate access to those parts of the records of the parent institution which it needs in order to manage its side of the partnership.

Where the partnership is a 'validation' rather than a 'franchise', i.e. an agreement to confirm only the standard of the final awards without controlling the detailed syllabus, the parent institution may feel that it only needs to keep the barest of records, and call on the partner college for any more detailed management information. The basic record would appear to be just sufficient personal information to enable a correct invoice to be issued: ID, name, course and such other items as are imposed by the nature of the charging mechanism (e.g. mode of study).

7.7 Archiving

In due course every institution must face the issue of archiving its records. While the student is still actively studying, the institution needs the fullest possible detail; once the student has left the need for this detail diminishes. At first the full record should be kept, at least until such time as it is certain that there can be no more appeals, or queries about the student's eligibility for any rights or awards.

Once this safety zone (e.g. about six months) has passed, and the final statutory return involving the student has been submitted, the amount of detail can be drastically reduced. Even where the mass storage of archive information is affordable and compact, it is clear that there is no point in keeping every detail for ever. However tempting it is to the historian and archivist to hoard it all just in case it yields fascinating analyses for sociologists a hundred years or more in the future, based on a yearning for similar data from the early years of the ancient universities, the argument does not hold water: the explosion in student numbers since the mid-twentieth century makes the amassing of such data unrealistic and probably of little value in the long term.

The institution must therefore address its own needs when considering its primary objective in archiving. The following are the most obvious needs and uses of an archive:

- enough data to verify a student's qualifications;
- enough data on modules to verify transcripts from many years before;
- enough data to ascertain a student's eligibility to undertake further study ('top-up' courses, postgraduate study, etc.);
- enrolment and year-end snapshots for analyses of intake and completion trends across many years.

Some of these are easier to manage in computerized archives than in manual records. Some are useful for a longer period: personal data are probably worth keeping in reasonable detail for about ten years; statistical snapshots can remain useful for twice that period.

What is retained on the archive will depend on what analyses the institution finds useful. The basic personal information after about ten years could well be restricted to: full name, date of birth, sex, start date, end date, all qualifications and classifications, last known address. What can be dropped is all information on finance, attendance, and probably also the module marks. Cohort analysis becomes of little value once the courses have evolved and the syllabuses are too different for comparisons to be meaningful. The provisions of data protection legislation must also be borne in mind if it prohibits the storage of obsolete data which are not usable for historical analysis.

The format of the archives is of little relevance, provided that they are easy to set up and easy to use. Non-computerized records tend to limit their own archives by their very bulk: annual and end-of-course weeding is the only solution, and should be drastic at about two years after the students have left. Archiving mass records to cupboards is a waste of time. Archiving to image archives is only useful for verification of documents, not for analysis.

7.8 Transcripts

Assuming that the institution's records hold all the information needed for a transcript, the format and content of the document still need careful consideration. Irrespective of whether it is called a 'transcript' or a 'record of achievement', the decision on the content must still be taken sensitively, bearing in mind the use which the student will want to make of it, and avoiding possible misuse for fraudulent purposes.

- The transcript should show all the modules and marks which were used to determine the passing and classification of the course and award.
- Showing all attempts at each module might be needed if the student's activities each year need to be certified.
- Showing only the final attempt at each module gives an accurate indication of what the final board of examiners considered, having discarded all earlier attempts.
- Showing the best attempt at each module is similar to the above: it depends on the institution's policy; the final attempt is not necessarily the best attempt.
- Including failed modules can reflect badly on the student, especially if the student feels that they became irrelevant when other modules were subsequently substituted for them, but conversely a student can still find the fact that a module has been studied (albeit not passed) of value when seeking employment, especially if the failure was marginal. In such a context the institution may wish to show the failed modules in a separate section entitled 'also studied' rather than 'failed', especially if the failure was condoned and treated as an adequate performance for some purposes (e.g. prerequisites).
- Showing results of ancillary modules can be misleading, especially if the institution allows students to take modules (e.g. as an associate student) completely outside their course.
- Showing the course for which the student was registered each year is probably irrelevant unless it is needed to clarify an otherwise inexplicable selection of modules; in most cases only the course title of the final course is relevant.

Unless all the above permutations can be managed for their various purposes, the most useful versions appear to be (a) all attempts, (b) just the best attempts, (c) just the passes.

What definitely ought to be included for each year is whether the course was studied at the institution itself or at a partner college. This is not only a good way of recognizing the contribution of the respective institutions but it also prevents students from misrepresenting their whereabouts each year; this can have serious legal implications if one of the partners is in a different country. The same may apply to any notes about whether the course (other than language courses) was delivered in a language different from that of the parent institution itself: studying in a particular country, or for the award of an institution in a particular country, could be misrepresented as implying competence or fluency in the language of that country.

The question of what information should be included in references is covered in Chapter 9, section 9.7.

8

FINANCIAL AND LEGAL OBLIGATIONS

Why obligations work in both directions, external constraints and the role of the courts.

Obligation is a pain.

(Samuel Johnson, *The Rambler*, 15 January 1751)

8.1 What are the obligations?

In most instances legal and financial obligations work both ways within higher education: there are obligations equally on students and on the institution. Some parts of educational administration are very tightly constrained by external factors, not least general legislation. This applies particularly to areas outside student administration, such as staff and finance. This chapter makes no attempt to discuss transient statutory orders, or specific legal obligations contained within legislation. First, a volume such as this could do no more than scratch the surface of some very complex areas of law; second, some of the statutory provisions are too liable to change to be suitable for coverage here. Those interested in detailed aspects of administrative and financial law are referred to the appropriate specialist services – and see Farrington (1998), Palfreyman and Warner (1998); also McEwan (1996), Hyams (1998). The notes which follow therefore cover only such aspects as are likely to arise in the normal duties of a higher education manager or administrator.

8.2 Financial administration of student records

Finance is one of the principal areas in which student records systems encounter legal considerations. This is not because there is anything particularly complicated about student financial matters, but because once money is involved the administration has to take into account legal liabilities, contracts and debt management, to say nothing about accounts, auditing requirements, probity, security and fraud.

Financial systems, and finance administration itself, is a vast area far too complicated to cover in any detail within the confines of this book. Furthermore, finance administration differs from academic administration, and student administration in particular, in that it is strongly influenced by legal, statutory and professional requirements: higher education institutions may have total autonomy when designing degree structures, but very little scope for flexibility when accounts are prepared. However, student records systems have to interface intimately and inextricably with the institution's financial systems for the purpose of invoicing: not only tuition fees, but also residences, materials charges, examination fees and many, many more things.

In the early years of computerized administrative systems, the invoicing system was often run as a separate operation from the student records. This, though probably unavoidable given the technology available at the time, led to tremendous problems of reconciliation between the two systems. Lengthy, detailed and tedious procedures had to be set up to enable manual checks to be made, comparing the names on the student records system with those on the invoicing system, before a final agreed student count could be presented to the institutional management, or the funding authority. On many occasions there would be significant differences of opinion between finance and registry concerning the number of students, and, just as crucially, about fee income projections based on these numbers.

To run modern systems in a way which still perpetuates this need is not a good idea at all, though it is still fairly common to find student invoicing being treated primarily as part of the accounts and sales/ledger, with a reconciliation with student records as an optional extra, or even as an afterthought. The systems ought to be fully integrated: that does not mean that they have to be on the same machine, or use the same database, but it does mean that for invoicing purposes the entirety of the combined data-sets must be fully consistent before invoices are issued. To this end the finance system should not duplicate data primarily held on the student record (such as course, mode of study), unless they are copied direct from the latter for convenience of local processing.

It is not just computer systems which risk being confused if the finance system is run too separately from the student records system:

students too can find it confusing. Students have a right to see 'the administration' as a seamless whole; to make them responsible for conveying information from one part of the administration to another is unacceptable. For example, if a student needs to register for an examination, and this involves paying a fee, the student ought to be able to do both at the same time, in the same office, to the same member of staff. This can present tricky logistics for the institution, but must be the ultimate aim. In terms of consumer relations, to ask a student to pay in one office (the cash office, for example) and then carry the receipt back to the examinations office, is a sure recipe for mistakes, misunderstandings, or simple fraud – and certainly for irritation and frustration for the student!

8.3   Student debtors

One of the effects of treating student invoicing as simply a normal part of the general institutional financial system is that student debts are treated in exactly the same way as debts by any other person on the system. The institution has to be sure that it is comfortable with this assumption. As a significant proportion of income is drawn from direct payments by students, it is probable that, unlike under earlier financial regimes where student fee contributions were a minor part of the income, the institution cannot afford to do otherwise. This reinforces the concept of the 'student as customer' or 'student as consumer': the student's relationship to the institution is just that of any other customer in a commercial transaction, in that non-payment results in both withdrawal of service and demands for payment of outstanding dues.

Many staff, particularly academic staff, have not yet come to terms with this change in relationship. When almost all institutional income came from the government (directly or indirectly), and student debts derived almost entirely from residential dues, institutions usually saw no reason to impose any academic sanction, such as termination or suspension of enrolment. Academic tutors, for fully admirable reasons, see the role of the institution as philanthropic rather than commercial, and their own personal role as purely academic rather than administrative. The undesirable side-effect of this is that some tutors see no reason to enforce financial sanctions: comments such as 'it's my job to teach them, it is no concern of mine whether they have paid their fees', are all too common. In turn, imposition of sanctions such as withdrawal of enrolment can cause conflict between the administration and the student's tutor: the former pointing out that a significant proportion of the latter's salary is drawn from direct fee income, and the latter accusing the former of sheer bureaucracy out of place in a seat of learning.

A similar attitude is adopted by many students: there is a marked reluctance to see the payment of tuition fees as the same type of financial transaction as buying any other service outside education. There is surprise when non-payment results in sanctions. To a large extent this is understandable in the context of the development of higher education, particularly in the United Kingdom. The tradition has grown up (albeit relatively recently, i.e. the second half of the twentieth century) that the educational service is provided and paid for by the government, and that the student's own contribution is an optional extra, the 'icing on the cake'. This is no longer the case. A corollary of this is that among those students who realize the importance of prompt payment of dues there is a marked reluctance to enrol, since enrolment leads directly to an invoice, and invoices have deadlines, and missing deadlines leads to sanctions: delaying enrolment means, in effect, longer deadlines and postponing sanctions. Where students are particularly astute they can use this period to lodge their funds in high-interest bank accounts, gaining significantly from the institution's willingness to give extended deadlines.

The institution therefore has a choice: to treat a student who has not paid the fees simply as yet another defaulter/debtor with all that this implies, or to treat them as partners in the educational experience who also have incidental financial commitments. As institutions have to become more financially dependent on direct student income, the former view is increasingly the only choice. There are two implications of this:

- Terminating or suspending enrolment ('terminating the contract') can have significant financial implications: the institution forgoes any fees due for the remainder of the period, probably has little chance of recovering the debts so far and may incur penalties from government agencies if the dismissal of the student has an impact on funding council targets.
- A contract has two parties: if institutions start to impose sanctions for non-payment of fees, students are correspondingly increasingly likely to make counter-claims for non-provision of adequate tuition as a defence for non-payment. Whether these claims are justified or are merely a means of evading commitments is a different question, which the institution must evaluate for each case on its merits.

The considerations above militate against simply treating students as debtors in the way a high street store would, but the temptation (however strong) to go to the other extreme and treat student debtors as somehow less serious than other debtors must also be resisted. As in so many other areas, it is the achievement of a meaningful and workable balance that is crucial: the financial integrity of the institution must be maintained, but the financial hardship of many students must also be recognized.

A very awkward aspect of using sanctions against students for non-payment of fees is any legislation which requires the sanction to be related to the charge originally levied. For example, can an academic sanction be imposed for non-payment of residence debts? Probably not, unless the student–institution 'contract' has specifically linked this 'punishment' to that 'crime'. Legal advice should be sought when devising this policy, as the interrelationships of offence and sanction can be quite complex.

8.4 Debts by student sponsors

In some ways more difficult to manage are debts by a student's sponsor. Should the institution penalize the student because of the sponsor's delay? If the sponsor defaults completely, or withdraws support, the solution is more straightforward: the financial liability falls immediately on the student, and the debt is the student's if the enrolment is to continue.

More difficult is late payment, or prevarication. In cases where the sponsor is a government agency, whether in the same country or some other one, the institution may feel that it can wait longer than it would with a student debtor, on the grounds that it is certain to get the money in due course. However, that is not always a certainty: it is not at all unknown for foreign governments simply to ignore repeated invoices, even accumulating several years' fees, resulting in students getting free tuition for their whole degree.

Where the sponsors are private or commercial, the institution must treat them in the same way as if the students were paying the fees themselves. Part of the reason for this is that in a large number of cases the 'sponsor' is a member of the student's family: a family business, a guardian or other relative, or a local sponsorship deal as part of a private arrangement. To deal with these sorts of sponsorships more leniently than students' personal liability is not only unjustified, but would inevitably lead to manipulation of the system by students who realized that feeding their fees through a third party, as if through a sponsor, would enable them to delay payment.

The sponsors also have interests: they (presumably) are keen that the student for whom they are paying is going to acquire skills that will benefit them as sponsors. The threat that enrolment will be withdrawn, whether made direct to the sponsors or via the student, usually makes sponsors realize that there is a real risk that their investment may be wasted.

The range of excuses presented by students and sponsors for late payment is enormous. One frequently presented, particularly by sponsors from other countries, is that the exchange rate is not favourable at the time of the invoice. The institution must disregard such requests: it is not part of the institution's role to arrange, to its detriment, financial transactions to the benefit of the payer; unless, of course, in the institution's judgement it is the only way of ensuring payment at all.

8.5 The student 'contract'

Much mention is made of the student 'contract' with the institution as a result of enrolment (Palfreyman and Warner 1998: Chapter 6; Farrington 1998: Chapter 4). A word of caution is needed, however: at the time of writing it has still not been *absolutely* confirmed by test cases whether a student enrolment is *really* a 'contract' in the way assumed above. The 'contract' argument may therefore be a little risky unless there are specific promises in the enrolment or recruitment documents. The 'contract' in the statutory higher education institutions and in the colleges of further education is probably more clearly in existence, and is these days increasingly frequently litigated upon in the courts (either as a contractual dispute in the county court, or as a judicial review in the high court). The 'contract' in the case of the chartered higher education institutions and the Oxbridge colleges is clouded by the concept of 'membership' of the institution and by the role of the 'visitor' in having exclusive jurisdiction over what would be a contractual dispute or judicial review matter in the statutory institutions. The precise legal position, in terms of both contract law and educational law, is too long and complex to be covered here, and the interested reader is referred to the books listed, and advised to seek legal advice if any transaction with a student is going to be pursued under contract law or referred to the visitor.

One aspect which distinguishes the student's relationship with the institution is that in most contracts it is clear who is doing what for whom. Students are different in the sense that they actually contribute to both sides of the contract: to get the best out of the tuition offered the student (as learner) has to contribute to group tutorials and other learning activities. This is quite different from the straightforward purchase of a commodity, which is an exchange of money for a product or service. In some ways it has aspects of employment law in it, since there is a continuous relationship between the work of the student and the work of the institution. On the other hand, one unique aspect of the relationship is that a student, having paid the required tuition fee, can decide to teach himself or herself using the library and other resources, eschewing attendance at all lectures and tutorials. If such a student can successfully complete the course, it is far from obvious how the role of the tutorial provision forms an integral part of any contractual agreement. The true relationship of a student to the institution is probably much better defined as 'client' or 'consumer' rather than 'customer': it implies provision of a service rather than a product, and a cooperative relationship not present in a normal shop purchase.

Notwithstanding the above cautionary note, there are clearly elements in the student–institution relationship which are very close to a contractual agreement. This immediately raises two questions:

- What does the student have to do?
- What does the institution have to do?

These questions are explored in the paragraphs below.

8.6 What can the student expect for payment of fees?

(a) Facilities

Yes. A student paying fees for a course must have the reasonable expectation that the institution has adequate facilities for a student to acquire all the knowledge and skills required to complete the course satisfactorily. This does not imply that use of these facilities is mandatory: if the students wish to teach themselves they may do so; this is, after all, the basis of many distance learning courses.

(b) Tuition

Yes. A student paying fees for a course must have the reasonable expectation that tuition and advice will be available, even if it is offered purely as a postal course. However, this is not to say that the tuition can guarantee that the student will necessarily reach a standard adequate to complete the course successfully. Nor does it guarantee that the teaching or learning facilities will be available on demand, or at times convenient for all students' alternative commitments. Much discussion has been held on whether universities, or any other educational institutions, are a place of 'teaching' or a place of 'learning'. An institution can provide all the necessary tuition, but it cannot guarantee that the student will learn anything – the 'horse to water' argument in pedagogical terms. The student must not assume that attending all classes and understanding the subject completely is all that is needed for a successful outcome: for this the student must demonstrate and be able to use that knowledge. Similarly, students are under no obligation to use the tuition offered: if they feel that they can teach themselves they are, in most subjects in most institutions, allowed to take that risk, on the understanding that they will have no grounds to hold the institution liable if they subsequently fail.

(c) Personal care

Probably. Students have a right to a safe place of study. They have not, however, any rights to demand levels of personal (i.e. non-academic) support and care over and above those of any other service provider. Most institutions, though, take a much more supportive and philanthropic point of view. To a large extent this is the result of many centuries of tradition in which the institution was acting *in loco parentis* and was responsible for the welfare and safety of its charges. This is no longer the case, at least in higher education: almost all students are past the age of majority, and are responsible for their own welfare. Notwithstanding this, it would be a poor institution which did not provide significant advice to its students both on academic and on non-academic matters: most institutions have pastoral care provision for their students' personal problems, and extensive services for advice to students on course choice, module selection and careers destination. What must be understood, however, is that these are fringe benefits: they are not part of the core service of the institution and many institutions could be very successful, with many happy and successful students, even if none of these services were present. However, these fringe benefits are what mark out an institution as being an attractive place at which to study. It is the difference between a corner shop and a warehouse: buying prepacked self-assembly furniture is much less enjoyable for most than selecting and trying out a new product delivered to your specification following a detailed exploration of your needs with an understanding sales advisor.

(d) Assessment

Yes. Students should expect as a right to be assessed fairly, and on subject matter which it is reasonable for them to have learned while on the course. However, this does not imply that all topics covered in the syllabus will appear as questions in the assessments, nor conversely that there will be no questions on topics not directly taught in the syllabus. This approach is more common in subjects where the examination assesses knowledge over the whole subject rather than module by module. It would, of course, be unwise if the examination questions bore too little similarity to the content of the lectures.

If students have suspended enrolment for a period between the teaching and the assessment, they are usually felt to have a right to be assessed on the syllabus as originally taught to them, rather than as it may have evolved in the meantime, even if that means that the institution has to set them a special paper. This is probably more a humane convention than a legal right.

Students from other countries do not have a right to take their examinations in their home country. This question arises most frequently in the case of resits during the summer vacation or during a year away. The institution may regard it as good 'customer care' to try and arrange this facility, but it is not a right: the institution has the power to hold its examinations at whatever time and place it deems appropriate, and the students are expected to make themselves available for assessment, not the other way round. Students who are due to return for the next year (even if subject to passing these examinations) should be expected to return early for the examinations; more sympathy may be extended to those who have to take the examinations in the middle of a full year away, and it might, for example, be deemed harsh to make a student return from the other side of the world for a single examination.

(e) Results

No. Students are not guaranteed that they will succeed on their course. All that should be guaranteed is that a student with the right abilities will have a reasonable chance of being able, using the facilities and tuition available, to gain a successful level of knowledge and skills by the end of the course.

Nor are they entitled to be given their results if they have not fulfilled their part of the bargain. If students have not paid all fees for tuition, residence, etc., they should not be felt entitled to be told the outcome of their examinations. In one sense the withholding of the results can be seen merely as a very strong leverage on the payment of any outstanding dues. In reality it is more than that, however: it is the completion of the agreement brought about by both sides fulfilling their obligations, and this final stage on the part of the institution cannot be carried out until and unless the earlier stage (payment) has been performed by the student. It is therefore more about completion of the contract than about sanctions and leverage on debts. The above has not been fully tested in the courts, however.

8.7 Who does the chasing?

(a) The central student administration

The central student administration is normally the support department most likely to be charged with the task of ensuring that internal procedures are enforced. In the case of academic and internal administrative regulations this will usually be the registry.

This is inevitable: it is after all the role of the central administration to enforce the academic regulations and procedures. It does, however, have the unfortunate effect that students then see the central administration as an intrusive and possibly heavy-handed bureaucracy, remote, insensitive and not particularly worried about the timing of its actions (e.g. in the middle of examinations). Such is the fate of all enforcers of regulations. The only time when they are visible to their charges is when they have to enforce something: from the tedious but important act of enrolment right through to the unwelcome intrusion of disciplinary action.

It is an unfortunate fact of life that, however philanthropic, kind and flexible an administration wishes to be, there are significant numbers of students who will misuse this flexibility as a means of avoiding sanctions. To a large extent this epitomizes the changing role of higher education. In the days of small and intimate institutions, where everyone knew everyone else, a particular kind of relationship existed in which every person (student, academic, administrator) knew and respected the role of the other. In the days of mass higher education, with students regarding themselves as customers or clients, and more and more of the academic staff seeing their employment as a job rather than as a vocation, there are increasingly few qualms on the part of the students (and some staff) about finding ways of getting round the regulations (or even, in some cases, of thwarting them), as if it were some sort of logistical game. All of this forces the administration to be more formal, less flexible and therefore to appear less sympathetic; the regulations have to be more pedantically detailed in order to avoid innocent, mischievous or pernicious mis-reading of what should be clearly obvious in that context; procedures become more and more bureaucratic in order to cover the institution against any future appeals; the administrative staff appear more and more police-like, intrusive, remote and unfriendly.

All of this is a great shame, but it is not unique to educational establishments, so higher education institutions simply have to adapt to a more litigious and game-playing clientele, and recognize that this alienates their supposed customers, and their intermediaries the academic and local administrative staff.

There are certain strengths to this, however. It can often force an institution (in all its manifestations) to tighten up what could other-wise degenerate into sloppy and inequitable practices, sometimes bordering on favouritism, bias or prejudice. If a process or decision will have to be defended it certainly increases the care with which it is argued and documented, albeit that the outcome may be identical and the bureaucratic load made more onerous. In these circumstances the academic administrator can hope to be recognized as having to carry out an unfortunate but necessary duty for the eventual benefit of the institution. The legal right to carry out these duties is implicit in the administrator's employment.

(b) The central finance department

The central finance department suffers most of the features described above, but has one great advantage over the academic administrat-ive departments. Students and academic staff accept that financial rigour is bound up strongly with legal and statutory requirements, and the unquestionable demands of financial probity. It is accepted that many of these are not negotiable in the way that local academic regulations can be. Certainly there can be discussions about whether a student is liable to a particular fee, but once the liability is estab-lished there appears to be less challenge to the rights of the institu-tion to enforce the collection of the charge.

This distinguishes the enforcement of financial obligations from the enforcement of academic regulations: naturally it does not make their enforcement any more welcome, or the administrators charged with the enforcement any more popular with those being subjected to their actions. In fact it can have the opposite effect: because the financial administrators have recourse to legal financial requirements they can come over as uncaring 'bean counters', whereas careful academic administrators can present their actions as a desire to help but an inability to justify special treatment. As with academic administrators, the legal right of finance staff to impose sanctions and enforce obligations is implicit in their employment.

(c) Tutors

The way in which tutors approach finance departments differently from the way they approach academic administrators reflects the different functions mentioned in (a) and (b) above. The advice of the former is sought in terms of 'How can we avoid, minimize or delay payment?' and of the latter in terms of 'How can we reinterpret the rules to the benefit of the student?' This in turn affects the way in which tutors represent these two central offices to their tutees: finance rules are seen to be fixed, academic rules are felt to be flexible and therefore arbitrary.

(d) Administrators in academic departments

The role of the local departmental administrator can be very difficult in these matters. On the whole this is not affected by the extent to which the institution is centralized or decentralized, unless the decentralization is total. Any enforcement of regulations or financial obligations which have been decided by the central authorities highlights the role of the local administrators as intermediaries. Typically they will have little or no discretion whether the sanction should be imposed, or the imposition pursued. Even though local administrators are usually much nearer to the students than their central counterparts (who may rarely meet students apart from at enrolment), they can be seen as the lackeys of the central administration, with all the negative connotations described above. On the other hand, they can also be seen by students (and academic staff) as local champions against the unmoving and unfeeling central bureaucracy.

Those charged centrally with the enforcement of regulations and other discipline have to rely strongly on local administrators, even if only to ensure that communications reach the students. Local administrators also frequently have to enforce any sanctions imposed, if this involves deprivation of access to facilities. Care must be taken to ensure that those whom the central authorities have charged with such enforcement actually have the power to enforce within their job description. It would be inappropriate to place a heavy enforcement duty on relatively junior staff in the academic departments: if they are in a vulnerable position while attempting to enforce sanctions they need and deserve the full backing of senior departmental staff and of the central administration. None the less, as administrators they have a clear right and duty to enforce the rules of the institution.

(e) Academic staff

The position, power and role of academic staff are interesting, in that they have changed significantly over the past few decades: whether this is positive evolution or deterioration is a moot point. In the very traditional role of the tutor there was no question of being asked to impose regulations or enforce sanctions: the duty of the tutor was to teach; it was up to the administration to decide whom they could teach. If students attended, the tutor taught them; if students did the examination, the tutor marked it. This view still exists, and not only with older academic staff who had their formative years in such an atmosphere.

However, there is a subtle change in the thinking behind this approach. In earlier times the justification was based on different roles and an acceptance of the need to 'protect' academic staff from administrative matters; in more recent times the very erosion of this protection from administrative matters, and the increasing administrative demands placed on academic staff, has led to an increasing resentment on their part as being seen as the policing arm of the administration. This can cause contradictions: tutors who on the one hand demand accurate student lists from the administration may on the other hand refuse to take any responsibility for barring from their classes any students who are not on these lists.

If such an attitude was based merely on the argument that the unauthorized attendance was the result of failure to keep the records up to date it would be understandable, but often it is also adopted in the case of students who have been debarred from attendance on disciplinary or financial grounds. This is very unhelpful, and very inconsistent: the tutors who have this attitude are frequently those who feel most pressured by overwork, yet by teaching a student who has been debarred for non-payment of fees they make the institution give the student free tuition, which further increases the financial pressures on it and on its staff. There is a conceptual failure on the part of such academic staff to link fee default with the ability of the institution to pay their salary.

The legal power of tutorial staff to impose regulations and enforce sanctions needs to be clearly defined in their job descriptions; this is particularly true for academic sanctions derived from local functions. If an institution is to avoid legal challenge to its actions, the tutorial staff must have clearly specified powers to impose any sanctions which are felt necessary (for example, for cheating or poor attendance). Academic staff should not normally be given powers to levy financial sanctions for academic misdemeanours, except under very closely defined circumstances. Far better is to give the academic staff the power, and indeed the duty, to report any student infringement of regulations to the central administration. This is not a question of sheltering the academic from the dirty business of administration and discipline, but to ensure that any consequential action is carried out by those steeped in such actions, and well versed in case lore, precedent and procedures. It is all too easy for academic staff, with the best of intentions, to say or write things to the student which are completely against the spirit or letter of the regulations; such misinformation can make it very difficult to reach a fair and prompt outcome. This does not at all mean that academic staff *cannot* have the legal power to carry out such actions: if the power is given to them, then they do have it.

(f) External agencies

External agencies do not have a role to play in academic regulations, with the exception of financial default. In appropriate cases institutions may wish to call in assistance from debt agencies or, following appropriate court action, even from bailiffs, as is their right.

8.8 Sanctions ■

The general question of the appropriateness of certain sanctions is covered in more detail in Chapter 6. However, two basic questions often arise in connection with the legal powers of educational institutions:

• Does the institution have the power to do it?
• Can the courts overturn it?

The answer to both questions is covered by the same point about the legal position of educational institutions at all levels. Institutions have the power to do anything that is legal. And since these rules are internal the courts cannot overturn them, except for a rather recondite feature covering 'reasonableness', established in *Theatre De Luxe (Halifax), Ld* v *Gledhill* [1915] 2 KB 49, and the 'Wednesbury unreasonableness' case, which covers legitimate but irrationally severe penalties (for example, a case might be made if the penalty for trivial plagiarism was expulsion).

When students enrol at an institution they must undertake to abide by the rules and procedures of that institution. Without delving too much into the vexed question of whether the act of enrolment constitutes a contract in the same way as a commercial or employment contract, it must be clear that by enrolling on a course a student agrees to be bound by, and to abide by, the academic regulations for that course: its syllabus, the assessment, the progression rules, the rules for successful completion and classification. It follows, therefore, that a student should not be able to challenge the outcome of these rules. Certainly a student can challenge whether the rules and procedures have been carried out as promised, and this is explored further in section 8.12, but that is not the same as being able to challenge the procedures and rules themselves.

Despite the apparent obviousness of this assumption, it is prudent for an institution to make the student's agreement quite explicit (see Farrington 1998: 402–3, for a model student contract). There should be a statement on the enrolment form, signed by the student, confirming agreement to abide by the institution's regulations (whether academic or other). If there is good reason why certain parts of the regulations do not apply to individual students or groups of students this should be reflected in special regulations: it should never be open to the student to exclude himself or herself from certain aspects of the regulations, as otherwise the situation would be unmanageable.

If a student is going to be able to sign such an undertaking with confidence, there must be an assumption that there are no hidden or unreasonable clauses in the regulations. Students must know enough to make a reasoned agreement, but clearly they cannot be expected to understand every last sentence in the regulations; nor can they have the right to demand and be given an unreasonably detailed explanation of every provision before signing the enrolment form. To this extent educational enrolments are still largely a matter of trust: students trust the institution not to have such strange regulations that they are always going to be innocently falling foul of them; were there such regulations they probably *could* be challenged in the courts as being 'unreasonable'.

The other side of this understanding is that the full regulations must be available to students if they wish to consult them during their course: by all means have a summary brochure for the students on the basic precepts of the regulations, but if they wish to explore the full regulations they have the right to do so. Copies must be available in easily accessible places (on-line, departmental offices, libraries, etc.), and administrative staff must be willing to explain individual sections to interested students. There is no legal consensus on whether students must be given a physical copy of the regulations at enrolment, although many institutions feel it prudent at least to give them a copy of the disciplinary regulations.

The method whereby the student agrees to abide by the regulations is much less important than the fact that the agreement itself is obtained, and is *known* to have been obtained. Agreement need not be in writing, although that is the easiest to manage; equally binding are oral undertakings, but these are less easy to prove. Electronic signatures (e.g. a student confirming acceptance of the regulations on-line) ought to be acceptable if there is adequate provision of security to ensure that it is indeed the student who gave the confirmation (e.g. passwords); this is an untested area of law, however, so it should be treated with caution until universally accepted protocols are in place.

Given the above position, it should be clear that an institution does indeed have the legal powers to impose and carry out the most frequent sanctions, whether on disciplinary or financial grounds:

- withholding an award;
- refusing re-enrolment;
- terminating enrolment.

These sanctions are discussed further in Chapter 6. What is worth noting here, however, is the possibility of withholding an award not as sanction against the student but when it is part of a dispute. If the student is contesting the award or, more commonly, its classification, the institution must consider refusing to confer it, and should make provision for this in its regulations. It does not make sense to confer an award if the student is still disputing whether it is the correct award, in two ways: it does not make sense from the student's point of view to accept an award which he or she does not believe is correct; it is not sensible from the institution's point of view to confer an award if this could be viewed as putting pressure on the student to accept the award under dispute. To confer the disputed award merely as a temporary holding operation is more likely to lead to confusion, and gives less incentive to either party to seek an early solution to the dispute.

What is less clearly defined is whether an institution can impose sanctions on students as a result of misdemeanour not related to their position as students at the institution. This arises most often in connection with criminal activities, but can also arise in connection with personal or medical conditions which some parts of the institution might feel render the person unfit to continue as a student.

Most institutions have a clause which enables a person's status as a student to be suspended or terminated in the case of 'bringing the institution into disrepute', but this should only be used with extreme caution (see Chapter 6, section 6.7).

A somewhat contentious (and largely untested) area is the extent to which an institution can change the regulations while a student is in the middle of a course. Regulations tend to evolve organically as new situations arise, and new loopholes are discovered. It would not be reasonable if students could insist on using the same deficient regulations as were in force when they first enrolled. However, there is more reluctance to change course structures after students have started the course, and academic departments frequently find themselves with several slightly different versions of the same course in operation at the same time, as successive cohorts work their way through; this can become unmanageable once students start mixing their cohorts through suspended enrolments, sickness and intercalated years. As in the instances mentioned above, it is prudent for the institution to inform students at enrolment each year that it retains the right to change regulations and course structures whenever it sees fit, on the understanding that this will not be too frequent or too radical. Similarly, the institution must make sure that it informs students whether fees can rise each year to allow for inflation; otherwise, legal advice has shown that a student can hold the institution to the same uninflated fee as they were charged in their first year.

Administration of regulations themselves can be troublesome for managers: too many or too frequent changes confuse and annoy staff and students, whereas leaving them static for too long enshrines anomalies and encourages clandestine 'local rules' in academic departments and boards of examiners, with all the risks attached to that should there be a judicial review (see section 8.12). It is also very rare to reach consensus in an academic community about what the regulations should actually be. To try to devise a regulation by consultation is as wasteful of time as drafting one in a committee; the only practical method is for the manager to draft the regulation entirely, argue the case in a supporting document if necessary and then present it to the academic board or senate for ratification. Circulating repeated drafts for comment is a recipe for lengthy delay, which is usually undesirable (but which can sometimes be used fruitfully: for example, to provide time for the issues to be fully absorbed).

One aspect where institutions might well wish to have more control over student behaviour, but probably cannot do so, is the question of attendance, or more generally of students' conflicting commitments, such as paid employment taken during term time.

Although a student's mode of study may be defined as 'full-time', and the institution may expect that this implies a particular level of commitment to study, there is, in most disciplines, no tradition of requiring attendance. In such circumstances institutions may feel morally unable to control what students do when not in classes: in fact they probably have no legal control at all. These are the sort of considerations which make many feel that the word 'contract' is inappropriate in the student relationship, since the student does not provide the institution with any sort of consideration (other than payment of fees) or service, and can therefore not be sanctioned for failing to do so.

An institution might declare in its regulations that a student may not be simultaneously enrolled on more than one full-time course, but beyond that it has no (and may seek no) powers. It may (and should) counsel students on the inadvisability of taking on external commitments, but if a student wishes to do so it is their right. There has even, in many cases, been a belief that a student has an exercisable right to be absent for the whole year and just take the examinations; the fee is then for the facilities (library, etc.), rather than for the tuition. On the other hand, the rising need for students to take on work to support themselves financially, and the erosion of the difference between 'full-time' and 'part-time', may pull against requirements for particular levels of attendance in favour of levels of submitted work and participation.

Some disciplines in higher education do require attendance: this is usually part of some professional body stipulation and is quite common in subjects related to health or teaching, where placements are particularly important. In further education there is more of a tradition of requiring and registering daily attendance. This may reflect not so much a difference of care about the students' welfare as the fact that further education has tended to deal with younger students for whom the institution may have a stronger duty of care. Higher education students may be regarded as adults and responsible not only for themselves, but also for the consequences of their own decisions.

8.9   External legal and statutory constraints

Institutions offering courses have to have due regard not only to the normal requirements of the sort of legal constraints described above. There are other external factors which may require courses to be constructed in a particular way, and over which the institution may have relatively little control.

One of the main non-statutory constraints on course construction arises with the involvement of professional bodies. Originally set up to guarantee professional standards in the achievements of courses completed by students, they have always taken a strong interest in the syllabuses of the courses themselves. There can be little argument with this in principle, insofar as it concerns the core syllabus, but it can cause some problems when the professional body also tries to exercise control over non-core components, or the method of delivery, or to insist on the presence of so many syllabus elements that the overall course structure would become inconsistent with that otherwise required by the institution's own regulations. For example, an institution may expect, or even require, students to take a couple of modules from subjects other than that of their main course. If there is no room for these ancillary subjects there can be a confrontation between the professional body and the institution about whose requirements have precedence. This can be unedifying.

Similar differences can arise over assessment policies. Some professional bodies have a tradition of not permitting resits in core subjects, or may require any failure to be redeemed by taking the whole year again until all subjects are passed at the same sitting. Some may differ in the handling of compensation or condonement for marginal failures: compensation means the treating as a pass of a failure in a subject if there is a good enough mark in a closely related subject; condonement means disregarding the fact that a marginal failure has been gained in a subject if the performance is deemed otherwise satisfactory, even if there is no closely related module to allow compensation as defined above.

The difference is not purely semantic: 'compensation' results in the subject being marked as a 'pass' (which is not the case), whereas 'condonement' honestly recognizes that a weak performance has been permitted to stand without pretending that it has been passed, but without prejudicing the student's right to pass the overall course. Compensation is perfectly valid in some circumstances, but not all: for example, it would not be comforting to be travelling in an aeroplane and learn that the pilot had a failure in 'landing' treated as a pass because of a compensatory very high mark in 'taking off'. Condonement should not be used for key skills or knowledge, but is very useful for ancillary subjects: for example, a student who makes an unwise choice of one free choice module and simply cannot pass it would be ill-served by a system that made this generate a failure in the course as a whole. By and large, the more restricted the choice on a course and the more highly prescribed it is, the more it is essential that condonement is available in non-key syllabus elements; compensation is less easy to defend if it results in a module or course element being incorrectly recorded on transcripts as a 'pass'.

A further risk awaits an institution which links a course directly to a professional qualification, i.e. a situation where successfully completing the course automatically grants a professional status. The risk here is that under the institution's regulations it might be quite possible for a student to carry a failed module and still get a degree or other award, but the professional body might deny this happening as part of the licence which it is granting as its part of the agreement. The student could therefore appear to have successfully met all the criteria for a degree but be rendered ineligible for the award because of the more restrictive rules of the professional body. When this happens it can cause considerable distress not only (of course) to the student, but also to the teaching staff. The best solution (which most professional bodies accept as legitimate) is to have a closely parallel course which can be conferred as a fall-back award, without the associated professional status. For example, if a degree in subject 'X' includes professional licence to practise in some way, with hardly any scope for failure or condonement, the institution should consider a parallel award for subject 'X studies', with no professional licence to practise. Clearly the professional body may wish to exercise some control over the precise title of these parallel courses, so as to avoid future misunderstanding or misrepresentation, and that should be respected.

The other main external statutory constraint on course construction is the government, for those courses where the government stipulates the precise syllabus: for example, teacher training courses. There is little that institutions can do about this, although there is still scope for fallback awards as described in the preceding paragraph.

Non-academic legal constraints arise in some subjects. For example:

- health and safety;
- courses involving working with children, where there is a legal requirement to check on whether a student has a criminal record;
- students who are under 16.

8.10   Legal requirements on records

There is no legal requirement to have student records in a particular format; in fact there is no legal requirement to have student records at all, provided you can submit the required statutory returns and justify them in some way. However, there could be considerable problems for the institution if its systems are not compatible with official returns to funding bodies, regulatory statistical agencies, tax authorities, etc.

There are considerable requirements controlling the format and content of financial records, relating to audit, probity, etc. There is very little of this that is specifically related to student records as opposed to any other sort of records, so it will not be covered further here.

Not so much a legal requirement, more a question of duty or courtesy, is the matter of confidentiality. There are certain requirements covered by data protection legislation (see Chapter 9), but these tend to be rather simplistic, geared to the needs of individuals. There is nothing particularly wrong with that approach as far as it goes, but it does not always cover the sort of cases which may confront an educational administrator dealing with students: the duty of confidentiality towards one student may conflict with the duty to protect the interests of other students, members of staff or even members of the public. Other aspects of this are covered in Chapter 9.

8.11 Involvement with the courts

Fortunately, educational institutions rarely find themselves in the courts, other than in debt cases. This is because, for the reasons described above (section 8.8), the courts will not interfere with any institution's academic decision provided its internal rules and procedures have been properly followed. The courts may become increasingly involved with claims for compensation caused by allegations of poor tuition or supervision. This is intimately intertwined with questions of whether a student enrolment is a contract, and whether tutorial support is a right or an adjunct to the offering of learning facilities. The legal position on this is evolving, and will not be covered in detail here (see Palfreyman and Warner 1998: Chapter 7). In the chartered universities such contractual disputes are dealt with by the visitor, whose jurisdiction excludes the courts (see Palfreyman and Warner 1998: 340–60 and Chapter 8; Farrington 1998: 216–35).

8.12 Judicial reviews

Judicial reviews are probably more commonly encountered than actual court cases concerning disputes over the 'contract' or alleging negligence. These are where a student claims that an incorrect outcome has been reached (e.g. a low honours classification) because the institution has not followed its procedures properly. If a judicial review is heard, however, the judge will still not comment on the validity or correctness of the outcome itself, but will decide whether the procedures were not followed as laid down in the institution's regulations. In these cases, it is very important to note that the judge will look at the regulations as written, and will disregard any undocumented 'custom and practice' which differs from them, but might not disregard any condensed version of the full regulations included in the course document (see Chapter 3); the existence of any such divergence will make for a rather strong case for criticism.

Similarly, a judge or a court will not pay attention to whether the outcome was just or justified: doing the right thing for the wrong reasons is no defence in law. For example, in the case of the review of an examination mark, a student may ask for a review and, despite not actually meeting the normal criteria for review, may none the less be granted one, even though it yields a negative outcome. If the student appeals against this unofficial review, and challenges any refusal by the institution to hear the appeal, the courts would prob-ably rule that the appeal cannot be held, but only because the original review was itself invalid.

Even if the judge were to feel that the outcome was the correct one, there may still be a judgement against the institution. It is very important indeed that both students and institutions realize that this does *not* mean that the institution's decision was wrong, merely that it was improperly arrived at. What such a judgement means is that the institution must reprocess the student's case: it may still come out with the same decision. If the same outcome arises when the case is rerun using the proper procedures, and using them cor-rectly, the student cannot claim that the judge's wishes have been ignored.

Judicial review is a two-stage process. First comes the application to the court for a judicial review to be held; if the court feels that there is a *prima facie* case to be reviewed the formal review will take place later. The institution can contest the claim at each stage. The application stage may be quite brief, so if the institution can have it refused at that stage considerable delay (and cost) can be avoided. Nevertheless, applications for judicial review must not be treated lightly, as a finding against the institution can be quite damning. Legal advice from solicitors must always be sought and respected, and barristers (preferably experienced in education cases) engaged for the appearances in court (see Palfreyman and Warner 1998: Chap-ters 9 and 20; Farrington 1998: pp. 236–42).

A review can take a very long time, and may call for very detailed copies of institutional records; evidence of procedures having been followed may be asked for in a level of detail with which institutions are not familiar. This means that procedures should be well documented, as should the fact that they were carried out. This can be done in the minutes of the relevant committees: for example, noting that 'mitigating circumstances were considered for student X'. As noted in Chapter 4, however (and this cannot be stressed too much), the court will not be looking at the outcome of the procedure, only whether the procedure was followed: it will not lift, or look behind, the veil of academic judgement.

A good example of the above point is the question of discretion. If a judicial review hinges on the question of whether discretion was properly exercised (for example, by a board of examiners), the judge will ask:

- where it is specified in the regulations that discretion is available;
- where it is explicitly specified in the regulations that discretion is not available;
- where discretion is available, whether it was considered in all cases;
- where discretion is not available, whether it was none the less exercised.

Any failure to consider discretion where the body is empowered to do so will increase the chances of a finding against the institution. Any use of discretion not authorized by the regulations will also probably lead to a finding against the institution. If discretion is considered but the finding of the institution is that no special outcome is justified, this will *not* be the cause of a judgement against the institution: exercise of discretion does not guarantee a different outcome. This point is often misunderstood by students presenting mitigating circumstances to boards of examiners: being ill during an examination does not guarantee that a failure will be turned into a pass; nor is the board failing to take the illness into account if it still feels that a failure is the correct outcome, or that a mark is left unchanged.

Courts have a special aspect of discretion which institutions need to be aware of: this is the concept of 'fettered discretion'. This means that the procedures for exercising discretion must not consist of rules or constraints which force particular outcomes. If this is done, then discretion is not being exercised, as the institution is merely following rules.

It is an unfortunate and sad feature of the above procedures that an institution can be criticized by the courts for diverging from its procedures in favour of the student. Discretion can be exercised only if authorized; therefore it follows that any unauthorized discretion is wrong, even if it is done with the best of motives. For example, if a board of examiners has no discretion about the criteria for a pass, but none the less awards a pass to a student with fail marks, other students who have failed may challenge the procedures on the grounds that there is no express procedure which grants this power, and there would be no defence against a question why the board felt it appropriate to arrogate such a power for one student but did not do so for other failed students. The correct procedure in such cases is for the board to make a recommendation to the vice-chancellor or principal (as chair of senate or the academic board, or equivalent) to set aside a particular regulation and approve a particular special outcome, in the light of particular exceptional circumstances. That is legitimate; simply deciding that a board has discretion is not.

8.13 Students' legal status

The position of students enrolled at an institution is not covered by employment law; nor is the relationship the same. This leads to some rather awkward situations for institutions when there is some challenge or question about a student's right to be in the country. For example, although an employer may be legally liable if found to be engaging staff who are illegal immigrants, even if unknowingly, an institution appears to be under no such risk if enrolling an illegal immigrant as a student. However, to show how intricate the workings of the law are, the institution could be at risk of a charge of 'harbouring' the illegal immigrant if he or she is occupying the institution's accommodation. This means that if the institution discovers that a student is an illegal immigrant it may not be under any obligation to terminate their enrolment; however, it could well be liable if it knowingly re-enrolled them for the next session.

As in so many cases, this amply shows that legal advice from experts should always be sought where court action could be involved. In-house experts (whether retained solicitors or academic lawyers) rarely have the breadth of experience to know the latest rulings on every sort of case that may come up like this.

8.14 Powers of administrators and managers

People appointed to particular posts in which they will exercise particular powers – for example, to discipline or to fine – will have those powers vested in them by virtue of the post itself. Some senior posts will have their powers by institutional statutes or regulations.

However, it is very common for the administration of these powers to be delegated to others, or to a committee. It is very important to take care that powers of delegation are exercised correctly. Delegation of authority can only be granted by the person or body in whom that authority is lodged; the person or body which receives these delegated powers cannot further delegate the powers or responsibilities to others. If it is necessary or convenient for further delegation to be carried out it must be referred back to the original authority. For example, the vice-chancellor or principal will usually have the power to expel a student or to refuse admission to an applicant. Frequently the vice-chancellor or principal will delegate such powers to a deputy or to a committee; if this is done the committee or deputy cannot in turn delegate the power to a person such as the academic registrar. Moreover, if the vice-chancellor or principal is granted these powers on behalf of a higher body such as the board of governors, even the vice-chancellor may not be able to delegate the powers; this will depend very much on the precise wording of the statutes and regulations.

The best way to enable the above to be managed, where it is felt more effective to carry out the action at a lower level, is to have a subcommittee or officer such as the academic registrar investigate the case and make a recommendation; to comply with the scope of delegated powers, these recommendations are not final but must be passed back to the person or body with the formal powers for the actual decision.

A frequent example which arises when managing students is the breach of regulations: the academic registrar can advise an academic department whether a particular case breaches a regulation, or can advise a student if he or she has breached a regulation; if disciplinary action is needed, however, the academic registrar will be unlikely to have disciplinary powers but must pass a recommendation to the vice-chancellor, principal or whoever has the formal power. This may seem a minor technicality, or excessively bureaucratic, but it is an important means of ensuring that powers are exercised only by those authorized to do so, to cover the institution against legal challenge and to ensure consistency of action with regard to any decisions or sanctions involved. It would be legitimate, however, for the academic registrar, in appropriate cases (for example, if the evidence was incomplete), to advise the student that there had been a strong suspicion of an offence (cheating, etc.), but that no action would be taken on this occasion.

Notwithstanding the above restrictions on delegation, it is usually permissible for the chair of a committee to take chair's action on behalf of the committee, but the action has to be reported (and possibly defended) at the next meeting. Particularly in respect of student administration, this can lead to quite extensive lists of chair's actions being received at meetings: for example, boards of examiners should receive a report of all changes or additions to their decisions authorized by the chair since the last meeting. These may arise from appeals, reviews, mitigating circumstances, discovery of lost papers and a wide variety of similar causes. If the committee is unhappy with decisions made on its behalf by the chair, there are administrative procedures for dealing with that which are not directly related to student administration itself.

8.15 Fraud

As well as fraud perpetrated by students when presenting entry qualifications, or in forging medical notes for examinations, there is a great deal of forging or faking of award certificates. Genuine certificates can be faked by amending the classification or the award and taking colour photocopies; whole certificates can be forged with relatively simple desktop publishing software. All instances of dishonesty should be pursued vigorously.

Students who commit a fraud while still enrolled can be dealt with under normal internal disciplinary regulations; students who have finished their period of enrolment but have not yet graduated can have their degrees withheld. What is more difficult to deal with is students who have left, or people who present bogus or faked certificates when they have never been students of the institution. If the person is a genuine graduate who has falsified their award the institution should consider withdrawing their award. This does not dispose of the certificate, but it means that any employer checking on the qualification will not only be told that the award shown on the certificate is incorrect, but will also be told that the person 'is not a graduate of this institution'. This sanction should, in appropriate cases, also be imposed on others involved: for example, a graduate who knowingly lends their certificate to be used as a basis for a fraud.

There is no obvious sanction against people who have never been students of the institution, or who left without an award of any kind. To sue someone requires that the institution has suffered some loss or damage. If a person gains employment by fraudulently claiming to have an award from an institution it is the employer who may suffer the damage or loss by engaging someone who is incompetent. It is difficult to see what damage or loss the institution has suffered by this act, other than, conceivably, corporate defamation at the suggestion that such a person would have graduated from the institution. Most institutions find that they cannot realistically take any action against the perpetrator, although they can ensure that the employer is informed of the worthlessness of the person's alleged qualification. An institution may therefore decide that expensive action against individuals may be inappropriate, but it may feel differently if it is a matter of an entrepreneur who is repeatedly issuing bogus certificates for sale.

Without appropriate legislation there appears to be no legal redress against agencies which issue unauthorized copies of certificates, or even totally bogus certificates, other than perhaps infringement of copyright of certificate design. Because of the difficulty in proving loss or damage, the legislation against 'passing off' (e.g. using a name different from a product but only in such a minor way that customers think it is the real thing) cannot easily be used against 'degree mills' which make up fictitious institutions with a name very similar to a real one: for example, 'X University' when the institution's formal name is 'University of X'. The institution would have to prove that its registered name was universally recognized and therefore susceptible to such passing off.

It is, unfortunately, not only students who commit certificate fraud. There have been cases where members of staff collude with students to issue false certificates, often on misappropriated stationery. The staff involved should naturally be dealt with very seriously as a matter of gross misconduct (probably with dismissal) under the institution's staff disciplinary regulations, but action against the student can only be taken if it is known that there has been collusion. There have even been cases where the student was unaware that a fraud had been committed: for example, where a tutor has forged a certificate to cover up for an administrative mistake in the academic department.

9

CONFIDENTIALITY, DATA PROTECTION, REFERENCES

The importance of confidentiality in records, some basic aspects of data protection and their influence on release of data in references and other ways.

Wherefore are these things hid?.
(William Shakespeare, *Twelfth Night*, I.iii.135)

9.1 Confidentiality

Confidentiality of student information covers a much wider area than mere compliance with the data protection legislation. There may be areas of confidential information which are not covered by legislation, not least those items which are carried around as part of general knowledge about the student and which are never written down. It would be a poor institution whose only definition of confidentiality was to meet the base requirements of legislation.

It is not the aim of this chapter to give a detailed guide or reference manual on the legal implications of the data protection legislation. The main underlying principles common to various models will be considered, but only insofar as they have direct bearing on the day-to-day management of student records, whether computerized or manual. The wider issues of confidentiality will also be covered, whether or not falling within the remit of data protection legislation. Every institution should have a person designated to be in charge of the registration under the requisite legislation, whether national or international, bearing in mind that institutions with campuses or operations outside the home country will also have to comply with the legislation in force in the country concerned, including any aspects covering the sharing or transmission of data between countries. The institution's data protection officer should be contacted for advice on particular cases, or when more detailed guidelines are required.

It should be noted that higher educational institutions do not hold data only about students: there will almost certainly be records for staff, suppliers, marketing, guest speakers, graduates, external examiners and many other categories. The legislation does not distinguish between such groups: all are covered in the same way as long as they are actual living people (corporate bodies and companies are not covered in the same way, and often not at all).

Few countries have explicit legislation on privacy or confidentiality, but most do have legislation on data protection enshrining certain provisions covering similar questions. The United Kingdom's Data Protection Act came into force in 1984. European directives in the 1990s have not fundamentally changed the principles enshrined in the 1984 Act. Legislation in other countries does not differ radically in fundamentals. These may be summarized as requiring that the data must be:

- accurate;
- up to date;
- relevant to needs;
- in accordance with registration.

9.2 Being accurate ■

If any person or institution holds data about a 'data subject', the 'data holder' is required to ensure that the data are accurate. This may seem self-evident but is difficult to fulfil with total certainty. As with many aspects of this and other legislation, the law does not expect infallibility, nor does it set impossible expectations on procedures. There is an expectation of 'reasonable steps', which, while requiring that there should be satisfactory procedures and checks, does recognize that there is a limit to how close to perfection any system can be. In this context, it means that the institution should check the accuracy of the records regularly: this does not necessarily mean checking them with the student, though for many items (e.g. home address) that is preferable. The institution's procedures must not contain any laxity which could permit the holding of inaccurate data in any way which could damage the interests of the data subject (be they student, staff or member of the public). The holding of inaccurate data may not in itself be an offence, but any action based on inaccurate data which causes the person concerned to suffer a loss of any kind can certainly lead to legal action.

Many institutions carry out a basic check of personal information with the people on their records on a regular basis: for example, at student enrolment each year, or circulating staff with a summary of their record. This is sensible for personal information such as details of address or sponsorship; it ought not to be necessary for data generated by internal procedures (assessment marks, etc.), but it can actually be a reassurance to students and staff if all their data are available to them for checking. It has to be borne in mind that there is no such thing as 'secret computer data': all computerized data (and in some legislation all manual data too) must be supplied to the data subject if they make a request under the legislation. Such openness of data records can also, in the case of assessment, reduce the number of appeals and challenges from students who fear that their poor classification may be generated by faulty data.

9.3 Being up to date

As with 'accuracy', this seems self-evident, but is similarly difficult to ensure completely. People's information is always changing, so any computer record of their data is also likely to be out of date very soon after it has been stored. Legislation does not require constant updating of records, only that the data should be as up to date as is reasonably practical. The scope of this will vary with the data concerned: sponsorship details and home addresses can probably be checked once a year, but term addresses may need checking each term, and any attendance records every day. Student status should be updated each time it is known to have changed, allowing for any unavoidable time-lag between the change of status and the opportunity to record the change. This sounds rather subjective, but common sense usually prevails: for example, if you send a student an important letter to a home address which has not been checked for three years you may be held culpable for using out of date information if it leads to the student being unable to respond; if a student's status changes at a board of examiners but cannot be entered in the records for a week or so there would be little risk of liability *unless* in the meantime a decision was made on the basis of that student's status without checking to see if it had been changed at any recent boards of examiners.

Most legislation includes an exemption from the requirement to keep records up to date if they are used as archives, and statistics based on the position at a particular point in time. This presumes that these records will always be used in this way: if they are merely back-ups which could be used to reinstate a record which was supposedly current, they would immediately need to be checked to ensure that they were up to date.

9.4 Being relevant

Universities and colleges are educational institutions. They are also businesses. They will have all the normal records which any large business will have. However, their core business is related to their academic work. This covers a wide range of activities: students, staff, research, conferences, accommodation, retailing, security and many more. This, however, does not mean that institutions can be allowed, within the legislation, to collect and store information about staff and students which has no demonstrable connection with their stated business. For example, it would usually be difficult to justify the collection of data on a person's religious or political affiliation, or social and personal activities and inclinations. If the supplying of such information was made a condition of being a student or member of staff it could be open to legal challenge. Of course, if the nature of the establishment's activities justifies the need for such data (e.g. for a religious college, or a political training establishment), the challenge would probably not succeed.

Similarly, a person's criminal record is probably not relevant to the needs of most educational establishments, but is justified in cases where other legislation requires institutions to check on criminal records for particular courses, such as health care or working with children. As with so many other aspects of this legislation, there are few absolutes: the context may justify an action in one case and bar it in others.

It is not only the data which must be relevant: so too must the processing and purpose of the data. Institutions will hold each student's age, sex and (possibly) marital status. This is legitimate for the effective management of student business, and relevant management statistics. What would not be relevant would be to use this information to operate a student 'match-making' office or dating agency. Similarly, it would be of doubtful legality to use a student's date of birth as marketing information: for example, to send them details of the opportunities for holding parties under the auspices of the institution's catering department. These are legitimate activities in other contexts, but are not part of the institution's educational business, and could be challenged if the recipient found it objectionable; however, the challenge would probably fail if the data subjects had been informed, at the time the data were collected, that they would be used for such purposes, as explained in section 9.5.

The distinctions are not clear cut, however. It is probably legitimate to use information about dates of birth to write to students about the formation of a mature students society, or to staff about a pre-retirement course: these would probably be deemed to be related to the educational aims of the institution.

9.5 Being in accordance with registration

One of the basic requirements of the legislation is that there is some form of publicly available registration by data holders, stating what data they hold, and what they intend to do with them. Such a public register is only meaningful if it conforms with what the data holder actually does hold and do. These registers are of necessity fairly broadly defined; otherwise they would need to consist of a full specification of the entire business of the institution, all reports and analyses etc. None the less, an institution should not use its data for a purpose for which it has not been registered, and new activities should be checked against the registration to see if any parts of it need updating. It is very easy to drift from a legitimate use to an unrecorded use: alumni associations (see Chapter 2, sections 2.19–2.24) are usually set up directly from student results records, but are often used, as part of the association, for marketing purposes which will possibly not have been registered for the original student record.

The crucial point is that usually the legislation itself does *not* prevent an institution from collecting whatever data it wishes, or doing anything that it wants to with its records (provided that it is not otherwise illegal); all that is required is that these activities are registered. Using the examples from section 9.4, it would be legitimate to run a match-making agency, or use dates of birth for marketing purposes, if these activities were registered *and* if the data subjects were informed that these uses would be made of their data.

9.6 Release of data

Educational institutions rely heavily on the good will of their students and staff. It is therefore not only legally incumbent on them, but also sensible practice, to be very careful about whom student and staff data are released to outside the institution itself. Even if it has properly registered the activity, it would probably be imprudent for an institution to sell address information to mailbase agencies or insurance companies, or personal information to customer profiling marketing agencies.

This does not mean that institutions cannot participate in marketing or other surveys of their students and staff: the easiest (and safest) way of doing this is, rather than sending names and addresses to the surveying body, to undertake to forward the survey questionnaire direct to students from the institution. In such cases the institution should insert a covering letter informing the recipients that no personal information has been released to the body involved, and inviting them to participate directly with that body if they wish; any such tasks can be charged to the body concerned without compromising the probity of the records. Even for internal purposes such as the mature students society mentioned in section 9.4, it may be felt advisable for the initial invitation to be sent from the institution's academic registrar to the student on behalf of the society secretary, rather than merely giving the list to the secretary in person.

This appears bureaucratic and over-cautious, but people can be very sensitive about any apparent distribution of their data to third parties. For a mature students society it might be relatively harmless, but there are many potential political and social societies to which it would be most imprudent of the institution to supply information direct: for example, supplying a list of all students of a particular nationality to a student society for that country could lead to the list being misused as a means of keeping track of political dissidents. Even lists from foreign governments making innocent requests about the courses and registration status of their nationals may sometimes be covert ways of discovering what activities their subjects are involved with; if they are sponsoring the student such replies are legitimate, but otherwise it is more prudent to check with the student first whether they have any objection to the data being passed on, or to send the questionnaire to the students for direct reply.

More difficult to deal with are the requests for personal information received from parents, friends, flatmates and other contacts. No matter how distressing it may be, institutions do not have the right to pass on to such people, without permission, information which may lead to the enquirer learning more about that student or staff member than they would like. Students in United Kingdom higher education are almost all over 18, and all should be over the age (16) at which they acquire rights to run many of their own affairs. It is a regrettable fact that family rifts do occur, and not all students wish their parents to know their examination results. In some cases students may not wish their parents to know that they are even enrolled at the institution; this is particularly true where parents are divorced and the reasons for enquiring after students' information may not always be as innocent as they are presented. Parents are, for fairly obvious reasons, frequently upset at what they see as the institution's refusal to pass on legitimate concerns and requests. They must be handled sympathetically, but without compromising the student's basic right to confidentiality. Similarly, information about whether a person is a member of staff at the institution may not always be being sought for innocent purposes.

The institution must ensure that it does not lay itself open either to charges of unauthorized disclosure of confidential information, or to charges of aiding illegal acts such as harassment. The best procedure in all these cases is to undertake to pass on the request to the person concerned and ask them to reply direct; no guarantee can be given that the person will in fact respond, but that remains their personal choice and right. This is a particularly common procedure after the vacations, where casual student contacts may wish to continue temporary relationships. The function of the institution in such cases is merely that of a forwarding agency – it must not appear to be taking on the interests of one party, or act as intermediary.

Probably the only exception to the above is where the institution has good reason to think that the information is needed in a case of genuine emergency. Even so, caution should be exercised: the desire to pass on information about a family bereavement would be compelling, but it is not an emergency. Requests for information in genuine 'life or death' cases should normally be granted, particularly if they are from the official emergency services. It is useful, in such contexts, if the data protection or privacy legislation provides a clause which permits the release of information in an emergency if the data holder has good reason to suppose that the person would give their consent if they were present; this facility should not be used recklessly, however, or a legitimate challenge could be raised.

Particularly tricky to deal with are cases where the duty of confidentiality conflicts with a duty to others. These conflicts usually arise where personal information about a student is known which may affect the relationship with other students or with members of staff. The most common examples involve students with criminal records. A student with a criminal record may legitimately expect the institution to treat that as confidential and not pass the information freely around the institution. But what if the criminal record involves an offence against children? The institution should clearly take steps to try to avoid this arising as part of the student's course, but it may be difficult to arrange this without telling staff of the reasons. Cases are not always obvious: a student with a conviction for child abuse may be excluded fairly easily from a nursing course, since there are statutory provisions for this. However, the institution may inadvertently put the student into a situation involving children: for example, an art or geography field trip may involve working in a school or in a residential site also used by school children. The institution should draw up procedures for deciding exactly who can or cannot be told of the reasons, while also trying to avoid the implicit secrecy of these procedures giving hints about why a student's actions are being curtailed. Not only does the existence of such procedures help to ensure parity of treatment (insofar as these cases are ever similar), but it also helps the institution's case if there is ever a legal challenge about the way in which the decision was taken.

More complicated considerations arise when legal bodies are involved. Nevertheless, the same underlying principles must hold. Legal action is not the same as criminal action. Action by solicitors is not the same as action by or for a court. This means that letters from solicitors acting against a student on behalf of a third party must be treated in the same way as any other enquiry: the fact that a solicitor is asking the question does not remove the data subject's rights. Such requests should therefore be acknowledged but passed on to the data subject for reply. The most common cases which arise in this way relate to debts: the third party might be a bailiff, a landlord, a debt-collecting agency or simply a creditor of the data subject. The situation changes as soon as a case comes before the courts: in such cases the information should be provided, as otherwise an injunction could be served or charges levelled of impeding court business. Claims in letters implying that a court is involved should be carefully checked, and verification requested if necessary. It is very easy to imply that court action is in progress when this is not (or not yet) the case. Any cases involving the courts should be discussed with the institution's legal officer (e.g. the secretary or academic registrar) before responding. If information is given orally to police officers or other officials it is prudent to keep a record of what was said, to whom it was released and how the identity of the enquirer was verified, in case this has to be confirmed or justified later. As a common act of prudence it is advisable not to give out information direct to a telephone caller, but to ask for their name and telephone number and ring them back in a way which enables their identity and authority to be authenticated: for example, ask them for their switchboard number rather than a direct telephone line; if in doubt ring their manager and check why the information is needed.

It is possible to cause unauthorized disclosure of information accidentally. One of the commonest forms of inadvertent disclosure may not even strike the institution as disclosure. This arises with the disposal of confidential waste: not just through injudicious discarding of papers into bins, but also through relatively carefully managed disposal of confidential lists. Not all waste management firms which offer confidential disposal are equally good at actually destroying the papers given to their care. There is a large amount of subcontracting to third parties, and all too often papers which the management thinks have been consigned to a fiery death can materialize in landfill sites and public skips. The press often picks up these cases when they relate to government and health records: there is no reason to suppose that higher education institutions are any more careful than these bodies, and the same things probably happen more often than one would like to think.

Less risky if managed properly are the 'disclosures' of data on faulty disks which have been sent to disk maintenance agencies. These are usually more aware of the data protection principles and are possibly more easily controlled than general waste disposal bodies.

More subtle are disclosures by unauthorized users, or (more commonly) authorized users of the computer system who access parts of the record which they should not. Such access rights are often far too subtle to be controlled electronically. There is little to combat this other than eternal vigilance and scrupulous use of internal disciplinary procedures.

9.7   References and opinions

The considerations which govern policy on references have gained much greater legal foundation than those governing transcripts (see Chapter 7). The latter are assumed to be fact, whereas references are mostly opinion and judgement. For this reason, the format of references is often a compromise between data protection legislation which prevents anyone saying things which cannot be substantiated, and liability for giving full and accurate information to the person seeking the reference.

There is nothing in this specific to student administration: the laws governing data protection, honesty, libel, etc. apply as in any other form of reference giving. An institutional policy must be devised for both staff and students, as otherwise over-willing tutors may feel that academic references are somehow exempt from the normal constraints. To this end, accurate and trusted records are vital, since they remain the main resource of factual information which can be safely included in the references.

Mention has been made in section 9.6 of occasions where it may be legitimate to release information about a student without their direct permission. The giving of references may seem to be such a case, since the implied permission of the student seems self-evident. However, some legal cases have suggested that this justification should not be used excessively. The legal position is very complicated:

withholding information which could have enabled the person to gain employment could lead to legal action by that person; as could revealing irrelevant information which led to their not being offered a post. Conversely, withholding information which, if revealed, could have led to a person not being offered a post could lead to legal action by the employer. The same applies for references for situations other than employment (for example, for admission to courses or training). This legal and moral tightrope must be negotiated with extreme circumspection when providing a reference:

- nothing irrelevant should be included, especially if it is to the person's disadvantage (for example, reference to internal disciplinary matters);
- opinions should be avoided if at all possible;
- all relevant facts should be included (for example, examination failures as well as successes if the application is for another course);
- it should be made clear what the scope of the referee's knowledge is (for example, 'I know of no reason why this person should not be admitted' is safer than 'there is no reason . . .');
- if the referee cannot think of anything good to say about the person but sees no reason why the interviewer should be denied the chance of meeting the applicant, it is better to decline to provide a reference, unless there is the suspicion that employing or admitting the person would be positively dangerous (if the request to provide a reference is declined the potential referee should inform the person about whom it would be written, to avoid accusations of secretly withholding information).

These legal challenges have led to many references being anodyne to the point of having very little value. This is unfortunate but probably inevitable in a litigious society.

Whether in references or in general passing of opinions about students, all members of the institution must be made aware of the fundamental precepts of libel, slander and defamation. These are not always in accord with what non-lawyers might consider common sense, but it is certainly a good starting point to assume that it is risky to say anything about a person to a third party which one would not say to the person himself or herself.

9.8 In short . . .

The above considerations sound complicated, and can indeed be very complicated if courts are involved. Particularly in court cases, common-sense interpretations and assumptions are not always confirmed by the law. The best advice for any administrator or manager (or any other staff), in matters concerning data protection and privacy, is: if you would not like it to happen to you, it is probably open to legal challenge if you do it to someone else. See Palfreyman and Warner (1998) on data protection (pp. 166–8), and on references (p. 94), and, similarly, Farrington (1998: 548–53 and 373–5, respectively).

AFTERWORD: THE FUTURE

I call therefore a complete and generous education that which fits.
(John Milton, *Of Education*)

As was noted in the introduction, there are very few rights and wrongs in determining the proper way to manage students in further and higher education. There is considerable discretion available to institutions as to how they manage their own affairs.

Greater conformity may arise from the inexorable pressures of mass higher education, the sharing of technological solutions or the demands of students to be seen as clients rather than passive consumers. What is certain is that the need to be able to respond to these demands quickly, efficiently and accurately will not diminish.

These factors put strains on educational managers and administrators. The availability of information technology misleads many into thinking that all processes are easy, and all questions can be asked instantly and completely; this is delusion.

Changes in the ways in which students are taught, and in which they themselves learn, affect the ways in which they are recruited, managed and seen through to the successful completion of their courses. What does not change is the desire to see this final aim fulfilled.

The thoughts of John Milton given above apply not only to the education itself, but also to the way in which each institution chooses to manage it: choose the method which fits your needs, and do it well.

REFERENCES

Ainley, P. (1994) *Degrees of Difference: Higher Education in the 1990s*. London: Lawrence & Wishart.

Becher, T. and Kogan, M. (1992) *Process and Structure in Higher Education*. London and New York: Routledge.

Bell, E. (1996) *Counselling in Further and Higher Education*. Buckingham: Open University Press.

CSUP (1992) *Teaching and Learning in an Expanding Higher Education System*. Edinburgh: Committee of Scottish University Principals.

Earwaker, J. (1992) *Helping and Supporting Students*. Buckingham: The Society for Research into Higher Education and Open University Press.

Eastcott, D. and Farmer, B. (1996) Managing student learning. In D. Warner and D. Palfreyman (eds) *Higher Education Management: the Key Elements*. Buckingham: The Society for Research into Higher Education and Open University Press, pp. 205–16.

Farrington, D. J. (1998) *The Law of Higher Education*, 2nd edn. London: Butterworths.

Harper, H. (1997) *Management in Further Education: Theory and Practice*. London: David Fulton Publishers.

Harvey, L. (1997) *The Student Satisfaction Manual*. Buckingham: The Society for Research into Higher Education and Open University Press.

Haselgrove, S. (ed) (1994) *The Student Experience*. Buckingham: The Society for Research into Higher Education and Open University Press.

Hyams, O. (1998) *Education Law*. London: Sweet & Maxwell.

Jay, A. (1987) *Management and Machiavelli*. London: Hutchinson.

Lockwood, G. and Davies, J. (1985) *Universities: The Management Challenge*. Windsor: The Society for Research into Higher Education and NFER-Nelson.

McEwan, V. G. (1996) *Education Law*. Birmingham: CLT Professional Publishing.

Palfreyman, D. and Warner, D. A. (eds) (1998) *Higher Education Management and the Law: a Guide for Managers*. Buckingham: The Society for Research into Higher Education and Open University Press.

Piper, D. W. (1994) *Are Professors Professional? The Organisation of University Examinations*. London: Jessica Kingsley.

Ramsden, P. (1992) *Learning to Teach in Higher Education*. London: Routledge.

Roberts, D. and Higgins, T. (1992) *Higher Education: the Student Experience*. Leeds: HEIST.

Rowley, R. (1996) Student support services. In D. Warner and D. Palfreyman (eds) *Higher Education Management: the Key Elements*. Buckingham: The Society for Research into Higher Education and Open University Press, pp. 166–80.

Silver, H. and Silver, P. (1997) *Students: Changing Roles, Changing Lives*. Buckingham: Open University Press.

Smith, A. and Webster, F. (eds) (1997) *The Postmodern University? Contested Visions of Higher Education in Society*. Buckingham: The Society for Research into Higher Education and Open University Press.

Warner, D. and Palfreyman, D. (eds) (1996) *Higher Education Management: the Key Elements*. Buckingham: The Society for Research into Higher Education and Open University Press.

INDEX

STUDENTS
CHANGING ROLES, CHANGING LIVES

Harold and Pamela Silver

What it means to be a student has changed as dramatically as higher
education itself. It has always meant more than the formal academic
role, and this book is concerned with the changes in students' lives,
activities and attitudes since the period of student activism in the
1960s and 1970s. The authors have visited universities and colleges,
interviewed students and staff, and looked at the records of institutions and students unions. They go beyond past research concerns
with learning, attainment and statistics to discuss residence, students
unions, clubs and societies, the lives of different constituencies of
students, representation, leisure, hardship, part-time employment. They
consider the impacts of changes in size, funding, diversity, the idea of
community, and the definitions of students as apprentices, customers,
consumers, participants. They compare experience in the UK with that
in the USA. This is the first book to attempt such a wide-ranging
picture of students' lives into the 1990s.

Contents
Introduction: Students as a subject of research – Students in contexts – The
students – Living – Student life, students' lives – Action and representation –
The experience – Opinions and attitudes – 'The its worse' – 'Community'?
– Students as . . . – Appendix I: Interviews – Appendix II: Archival and
primary sources – Bibliography – Index.

224pp   0 335 19558 X (Paperback)   0 335 19559 8 (Hardback)

THE STUDENT EXPERIENCE

Susanne Haselgrove (ed.)

This book focuses on higher education from the student perspective. In particular, it examines the change in the UK (and other countries) from an elite model towards the USA model of mass higher education, and how this is reflected in student experience. Higher education courses are increasingly diverse in content, delivery and location; the student population itself has become more diverse; financial support and employment opportunities have changed; and customer care and a market focus are to the fore.

What are the implications for students, and how far have universities adjusted to their new constituents? This book tackles these issues. It approaches student-experience chronologically so is divided into sections on pre-entry, 'on-course', and on the period of transition to the next stage of their lives. By exploring a wide range of contexts, it is a valuable reflection of the overall pattern of student experience.

Contents

Contributors

John Bird, Martin Blakey, Chris Brannigan, Jackie Cawkwell, Clara Connolly, Gerald Crawley, Christopher Day, Dennis Farrington, Lesley Giles, Diana Green, Susanne Haselgrove, Mark Hadfield, Christine Henry, Tony Higgins, Ian McNay, Jill McPherson, Patti Mazelan, James Murphy, Sofija Opacic, Phil Pilkington, Phillida Salmon, Leah Sims, Ann Tate, John E. Thompson, Maggie Woodrow.

208pp   0 3335 19358 7 (Paperback)   0 335 19335 8 (Hardback)

STUDENT SATISFACTION MANUAL

Lee Harvey

This is a unique, clear and comprehensive do-it-yourself manual for all higher education institutions worldwide which intend to introduce a system of student feedback that provides management information for action. The Manual encapsulates a decade of experience of undertaking institution-wide student feedback surveys. It documents in detail all the stages of the Student Satisfaction approach, from student-generated questions, through questionnaire design, data analysis and reporting of outcomes, to the action taken by management to remedy concerns and to feedback to students about outcomes.

The *Student Satisfaction Manual* is an essential resource and blueprint for all higher education institutions which take seriously the needs and satisfaction of their students.

Contents
List of sample – Part 0: The student satisfaction approach – Part 1: Identifying key variables – Part 2: Group feedback strategy – Part 3: Designing the questionnaire – Part 4: Coding – Part 5: Piloting the questionnaire – Part 6: Administering the questionnaire – Part 7: Data entry – Part 8: Analysis – Part 9: Reporting the outcomes – Part 10: Acting on the report – Part 11: Feedback to students – Samples.

364pp   0 335 19779 5 (Ringbound)